Stuff my dad never told me about RELATIONSHIPS

Patrick Dodson

{ pause for effect }

Published by Pause for Effect Limited
709 New North Road, Auckland, New Zealand 1022

Pause for Effect books are available through most book stores and are also available in a variety of electronic formats. To contact Pause for Effect directly write to info@pauseforeffect.co.nz

ISBN 978-0-473-15312-0

Edited by Anne Munro McGregor, PhD

Printed and bound in the US and the UK by Lightning Source. Lightning Source UK Ltd. Chapter House, Pitfield, Kiln Farm, Milton Keynes, MK11 3LW.
Email: enquiries@lightningsource.co.uk Voice: 0845 121 4567. Fax: 0845 121 4594

National Library of New Zealand (Te Puna Matauranga o Aotearoa) data:

Title:	Stuff my Dad never told me about Relationships
Author:	Patrick Dodson
Publisher:	Pause for Effect
Address:	709 New North Rd, Auckland
Format:	Paperback
Publication Date:	8/2009
ISBN:	ISBN 978-0-473-15312-0

First Edition
Second printing

For Beccy

with thanks to
Chris for making me write

Noe, Naomi, Jasmine, and Emily for
their insightful feedback

Daniel for his house

Kevin and Lars for their process

Anne for her care and craft

Heather for her unconditional love

Contents

Forward

At the outset of this introduction I confess to being the author's son. I say 'confess' because you quite probably think I am therefore biased, and inclined to praise my father's work. Anyone who believes this obviously isn't a 21-year-old son reading his father's first book; I am in fact his harshest critic.

Patrick writes with the stern care of a father who hopes to multiply his own understanding and divert his listeners from the self-centered relational disasters that are so prevalent in our Western world. His scope is broad; he illustrates selfless love as it applies to men, women, the single, the involved, and the married. His perspective has found the foundations that seems to apply to all of us.

By combining personal experience, diverse scientific research, and spiritual principals, this book obtains a level of truth that resonates in my guts. Something inside falls into place as Patrick explores the chemical, emotional, communal, and spiritual elements that inform our relational choices.This book represents the author's simple, confident, and challenging perspective on a subject riddled with nebulous and misleading opinions. His thoughts on relationships are the most encouraging and provocative that I've heard, and he underpins each of them with practical fatherly suggestions.

I feel blessed to have a father who has so radically investigated the nuance of this subject, and I am privileged to recommend his perspective to anyone brave enough to reconsider the vampiric way we have come to see our relationships, and to work towards an unconditionally loving approach to the people around them.

Jordan Mark Dodson

Introduction

The picture on the cover shows my dad during one of his happier days. He's dressed up to be the best man at my uncle Johnny's wedding. Both of them loved the MG he's standing next to and I think they formed a bond over those cute little cars. They spent a lot of time together working on mechanical things and my dad even learned sign language (Johnny's deaf) to communicate better. But I never really knew him like this. The person I saw was always stressed, always on his way to work. When he came home, he often went straight upstairs to mess around with his HAM radio (the internet of the '70s). I didn't really know the man my mother loved. They didn't show much affection in front of us but I knew she loved him. When I was 11, his '58 Chevy slammed into another car moments after he left home. We all heard the crash but my mother immediately knew it was him. She screamed his name and ran outside. She had a connection that ran deep and a commitment that would have lasted his lifetime, if only he'd stayed around.

My dad and I never talked about relationships. He left for a year when I was nine, came back and left again for good when I was 18. Not a great platform for building trust or forming a dialogue together. Regardless, I'm not sure he would've had much to say on the topic. His dad got divorced, then died at the age of 52 from a blood clot in his left leg, which happened to be the exact way his grandfather died, at the exact same age. So entering into his 50s he was afraid, bitter, and struggling to care for a family of six. All this while working his arse off at a job that a guy who didn't finish high school was lucky to have. He was a relational time-bomb; I'm surprised he made it as far as he did.

From my perspective, it would have been impossible to even approach him and talk about what was going on in my heart. There was no way. By the time I was 19 I'd become so emotionally distanced from him, it seemed I had to figure out everything for myself. It's not that he wouldn't have had anything to say; it's that I couldn't imagine even asking, because to ask would have been to bring up a thousand other questions like, "Where were you when I was growing up?" I didn't have the grace or strength to go there. Apparently, neither did he.

Instead, I called on the profound wisdom of my drugged-up friends. You can imagine how well that went. I cheated my way through high school, had sex once with someone I barely knew and started to drink my way into the future. I joined the throngs of people running away from home to find a  different life, without a clue. My running took me to LA looking for a job, then joining a non-profit organization traveling around the world, all in order to find a different life, far away from home. I wouldn't have called it running at the time, but looking back now, I was a fatherless child trying to act all grown up. I could have used some more advice.

When I did tell my dad that I was going to travel around the world, on a ship, doing relief work, all he could say was, "You should stay home and get a job". Thanks dad.

Maybe it's easier for you. Maybe your dad's available, or your mom, to talk about the issues of your heart. Or maybe not. I've found that a lot of people never enter a deep conversation with their dads about the relationships they're in, or about to be in, or that busted thing that just finished horribly. As we grow up, it's really hard to talk as peers with our parents. It's hard because you don't know if they'd accept your preferences or priorities, if they really value your diversity. You might argue instead of discuss. Or like me, maybe you just don't like your dad's way of doing relationships... Perhaps it's hard to talk because you kinda know what you're doing isn't cool and you don't want to be accountable to him, or anyone. By the time my father left the second time, I had established a life without him. In doing so, I drifted into a lot of stupid things and didn't want his opinion about any of it.

I think I ended up in a kind of vacuum. No real fatherly input on one side, and a generation of confused peers on the other. My mom was available and always has been, but I needed a fathers perspective and it just wasn't there. So like most people, I just went with the flow. By the time I was 22, I'd developed some friends who weren't total idiots so that helped. But what I really needed was someone I could learn from. Someone who knew me, knew what I was about to go through, and had some real wisdom to share. I still needed a father.

Since that time, I've traveled to 30 nations and spoke to thousands of people. What I found is that my story isn't unique. It seems we've become stunted in our relational growth and are very much alone in our process. It also seems to me that we've forgotten the timeless truths which are so necessary to lasting relationships. I'd like to talk with you about this stuff. As a dad. Maybe it's just cathartic on my part (like the conversation I wish my dad had with me) or maybe I've got some really good advice from 28 years of practice. You can be the judge. But as a father, I'd love to be super honest and open about the process of relationships and, in particular, the power of unconditional love. Especially for those in their '20s and '30s who are right in the middle of learning how to love and be loved.

The downside is that I can't hear your part of the story. Instead, I'll have to share what I've learned through hundreds of experiences and conversations with my family and friends around the world. And while I'd like to approach you as a dad, my kind of fathering is very straightforward. This is not a soppy book with a bunch of cute anecdotes or clever principles you've heard before. It's pretty heavy duty and requires a lot on your part. If you're not ready, give it to someone else. Or read a few chapters and see how it goes.

This is a handbook. It's dense and works best if you read it straight through to get an overview, and then go back to walk out the steps that are relevant to you right now. I've left the margins really wide for you to take notes, jot down thoughts or make commitments to act on something you've read. We often read looking for "the secret" or some amazing answer to fix our problems. But really, there's nothing new under the sun; the trick is in the application. So use this as a workbook or journal and that'll make all the difference.

What I'd like to create for you, through this book, is *encouragement,* or the courage to do what you already know is right and what's best for others. I've found this encouragement from many people, a few of them fathers in my life, and would like to pass it on. Speaking of fathers, God has been a huge source of strength for me in terms of moving from a broken home and messed-up relationships to a healing understanding of unconditional love. Without the forgiveness, the wisdom, and the encouragement of God, I wouldn't have any authority to share my own experiences, because they would have been vastly different. At the same time though, I'd like to say that this is not a religious book. It's simply down-to-earth stuff that for me would not be doable without a spiritual connection. I needed something bigger than myself.

Finally, you'll find that I'm not a great writer, and as this is my first effort you won't read outstanding prose or a lot of brilliantly told stories, just a raw and simple approach to love. I intend to share my heart and wisdom, as a dad. I hope you can hear the kindness and vulnerability through the tougher passages. I hope you can feel the support during the challenges. And I hope you can see a better way through the mistakes of my process. If you were sitting in my living room right now, with the fire going, our big white dog (Chili) lying next to it, and my family bustling around us cooking something wonderful, I'd listen to your story and tell you what I think from a dad's point of view. Then we'd eat too much and watch a good movie... But since we're not together, please find some place comfortable, get something great to drink or eat, and I'll share a few things I've learned about unconditional love.

Part 1: Stuff we don't talk about

Where we are today:
Chapter one is about how selfish I am...

Chapter two talks about the meaning of attractions...

Where we can be tomorrow:
Chapter three covers the FLOW of unconditional love...

Chapter four shows how giving really is better than receiving...

One. I Love Me

To love oneself is the beginning of a life-long romance.
Oscar Wilde

The heart is deceitful above all things and beyond cure.
Who can understand it?
Jeremiah 17:9

This book is about unconditional love, and unconditional love is something you give. You don't fall in it, get it at first sight or meet it in a cafe one rainy afternoon... If you're looking for love, you never find it. If you try to take it, it evaporates. If you think it's out there waiting for you, it's not. If you think it's been planned for you, it hasn't. I'm sorry, but love can only be unconditionally created and given away, and this is the most amazing challenge on the planet. This kind of love heals and restores and blesses and fulfills anyone daring enough to have a go. On the other hand, anything less than unconditional love is a relationship that's slowly failing. And there's way too much relational failure going on. If you want to explore this, then read on. If you're looking for something easier, there are plenty of other books available about how great you are and how to get your way in love.

Here's the main problem: We love ourselves more than we love others. The "love" we do show masks the fangs we're digging into our victims, drawing the life out of them. We're nice, so people will be nice to us. We kiss to be kissed... And it makes sense; selfishness is the lingua franca of our time. We're spoiled or abused or both and we want something in return, dammit. Most of us have never been loved in a way that teaches us to love others, so we spend the rest of our lives trying to extract love and call it relationship. Extraction kills relationships. But regardless of your upbringing and history, your heart now has two choices: take love or give love.

So are you the taking kind, or more giving? Maybe you're a giving person and are doing your best, but others just keep taking from you. Perhaps you consider yourself reasonably unselfish but relationships are still not going so well, or are hard to find.

It's not your fault, and you're kinda tired of it.... What can I say, only you know your own heart. But if you're being selfish in any way, your relationships will reflect that. Whether it's a doormat kind of selfishness ("I'll be what you want if you love me"), or an overt selfishness ("What I want in a girl..."), the deep motivations we exercise to meet our own needs first will eventually kill the relationship. We need to change this. Not them, me.

The best place to start this process is to honestly look at your expectations.
- *What do you want in a relationship, and why? (Write this stuff down.)*
- *What really motivates you to pursue friendships or deeper relationships?*
- *What are some of your life goals and how do you hope others will help you achieve them?*

These are the things that motivate you on a day-to-day basis. They're probably very reasonable, strong ideas that you hold in your heart about how you would like to relate and be related to. They may even be noble and generous, but let's agree to be brutally honest about motivations and actions, because you can't be noble unless you start with how you *really* approach relationships with people in your life right now. Like with your father, mother, siblings, friends, and people you don't want to talk to anymore...

I think there's a gap between what we hope for in relationships and what we really do with them every day. There's an old story about a young man trying to get to a remote location. He pulls into a gas station to ask the ancient owner how to get from where he is to the place highlighted on his map. After viewing the map for a while, the old man looks up and announces, "You can't get there from here". You may want to give and receive love in a generous way, but you probably can't from where you're standing today.

So let's start with a quick audit on your ability to create and give love to others. Here are a couple of ways to look at it.

1. Internal influences: why we need to be loved sooo much
My dad left home when I was nine. I didn't know it at the time,
but he took my heart with him. His leaving created a vacuum
that only he could properly fill. Parents have a massive job in
forming our relational foundations, and they do it by meeting our
basic needs. These are:
• **unconditional love** (pure, no agenda, not based on responses)
• **provision** (safety, care, resources)
• **value** (self worth, belonging, identity)
• **destiny** (based on your value, what your future could look like)

We're born with these basic needs and we spend our lives trying
to get them met. Blaise Pascal wrote of an infinite space in our
hearts that could only be filled by God.[1] I think this is true, but I
also think one of the main ways God meets these basic needs is
through our parents and how they model (or not) God's love for
us. So we learn from the world around us how to get needs met.
If I cry, my mom puts her breast in my mouth. Mission
accomplished. We act on what we learn and we develop habits.
As we grow older, the game gets a little more complex. If we run
fast, people clap (value). If we wash the dishes, we get an
allowance (provision). If we look a certain way, we get asked out
(love?). It's all pretty natural but for a lot of us, something goes
wrong. Promises are broken, people leave, selfish priorities
develop and pretty soon we're fending for ourselves. We start
our search for love and take what we can get.

When my dad left, something broke. His absence skewed my
orientation and my ability to give and receive love. It's just a
small part of my story, but added to other inputs like media (film,
music, books), the wolf pack at school, extended family
weirdness and cultural histories, my view of love and
relationships got really tweaked. The results can be summed up

---

[1] "What is it then that this desire and this inability proclaim to us, but that there
was once in man a true happiness of which there now remain to him only the
mark and empty trace, which he in vain tries to fill from all his surroundings,
seeking from things absent the help he does not obtain in things present? But
these are all inadequate, because the infinite abyss can only be filled by an
infinite and immutable object, that is to say, only by God Himself."
(Blaise Pascal, *Pensées,* NuVision Publications, page 101.)

in the words of one canny psychologist: "When a guy says, 'I love you', what he really means is, 'I love *me*, I want you'."

So I learned to love me. I know this isn't everyone's story, but if your needs aren't being met, then odds are your kind of love is the extracting type. As in, "I love me, and want others to love me too". It's not evil, it's just not gonna work. Even if you've had a good family experience, the gap in our heart is huge and needs something supernatural to fill it.

We need to be more aware of how and why we're relating to people. The following is one way to assess ourselves. It's a simplistic approach, and by no means exhaustive, but the idea is to try to see where we're at today, especially in regards to our *need to get love* versus the *ability to give love*. I have suggested a 1 to 10 scale to get a good picture. Please be really honest about this. Tell stories that draw out the details of how you really are with others, not just how you want to think of yourself.

A. When developing relationships, do you tend to be more...
1. Conditional ("they should be funny, cute, smart...")
10. Unconditional (you seek out people for their sake)

B. When it comes to provision (not just money, but time and care for people) **are you...**
1. Always in need (of others' time, resources, love...)
10. Always giving (out of your own abundance) **and not just to receive back**

C. In terms of the need for value, are you...
1. Always looking for affirmation (encouragement, praise)
10. Secure and confident (and therefore honoring others more)

D. When it comes to your future, are you...
1. Looking for a ride ("hooking up" to someone else's wagon)
10. Providing a place for others ('cause you know where you're going)

My "relational scale" at the age of 21 (three years before I got married to Heather) would have looked something like this:

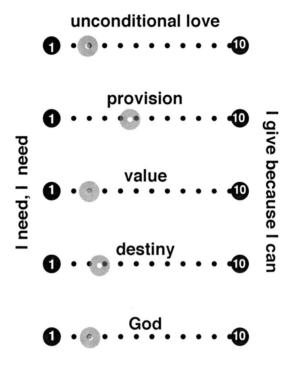

The last measure on the scale above is how co-dependent we are. Hardly any of us think of ourselves as co-dependent, but you may be surprised at how our sense of entitlement, or "affluenza",[2] has made us believe we desperately need something else to be fulfilled. Especially for the modern Christian. When it comes to provision, a lot of us have been taught that "God will provide", and so have lost a good work ethic. Or that "God will lead me", so we've lost the ability to plan or do research. The worst perception in this regard is that "God has someone for *me*", which leads to relational apathy. We don't bother to grow relationally because "God's in control". All this is

---

[2] "[...] painful, contagious, socially transmitted condition of overload, debt, anxiety, and waste resulting from the dogged pursuit of more." (John De Graff, David Wann and Thomas H. Naylor, *Affluenza: The All-Consuming Epidemic*, page 2.)

a kind of co-dependence (relying on God more than He actually intended), and it's not healthy. I think what God may be looking for is an inter-dependence, which we'll discuss later. But the question right now is: Are you looking for someone else to meet your needs, or do you create love that blesses others? On a scale of 1 to 10, are you co-dependent on God and others, or are you doing your part?

Most of our relational behavior is reflected in this overall scale. I was definitely more on the "I need, I NEED" side of life and, as a result, pursued people with a selfish agenda. There were some areas I was okay in. For instance, my dad worked really hard to provide for us, and my mom is the most generous person I know, so when it comes to provision, I'm a little more generous than needy. But in other areas, like value or unconditional love, I was really weak. I just didn't have the model or the understanding. So it wasn't just that I loved me, but that I needed everyone else to fill this huge hole. And I mean a massive vacuous cavern.

2. External influences: why you love you so much
There's already a lot that's been said about the Hollywood portrayal of love. Guy meets girl, they like each other, guy loses girl, they find each other again blah blah blah. It's cute and for some reason it keeps making money and therefore stays on the screens subtly influencing us. But like advertising (look and act this way to be happy), publishing (teen vampire versions of love) and pop music (love made simple for 13-year-olds), media culture has only a limited effect on us. What really shapes our thinking in this area is history.

A few years ago, I learned of a perspective on recent history that's made a lot of sense. It shines some light on how lazy and completely selfish we've become. The theory is about four generations of decline. For the most part, this is a Western model, but you may find this applies to your own culture too.

The **First Generation** were people in the '30s who responded to the crisis left by the previous (fourth) generation. Churchill, Stalin, Hitler, MacArthur, Roosevelt, etc., had to clean up the mess left by the generation before them who spent the life out of the economy and created next to nothing in return (sound familiar?). For instance, Germany in the early '30s had such massive inflation, you had to wheelbarrow 1,000,000 Deutsche Mark to the store to buy a loaf of bread.

The **Second Generation** had to deal with the loss and mass destruction of WWII and worked their arses off to rebuild. They learned the value of hard work and the need to invest in the future, to make plans and stick to them. They lived simply so the next generation could have it better.

The **Third Generation** took their parents' advice and did live better. They started to live off the fat of the land and shifted from a community orientation to making themselves happier. They started "day trading" in the stock market, built strip malls, cheap houses, and software startups to make some easy money. Then these guys had children: you.

The **Fourth Generation** (in the West) has never been in a war for their lives or survival as a nation (sorry, hi-tech "preemptive" wars over oil don't count[3]). For the most part, you Fourth Generation types didn't have to work really hard to survive or rebuild your city's broken walls. In fact, the three generations before you did their best so you didn't have to deal with the same hardships. The upside is that you now have more expendable time and cash than any other generation in history. The downside is that it's been so easy for you to become lazy and selfish. Things have been so laid on for you, relationships become something you deserve, just like everything else.

I think that the hard work put in by these previous generations has created a kind of playground rather than a community. Instead of building value in their neighborhood (jobs, knowledge, better health), most people are simply consuming whatever's around them. Eventually, all this leads to a crisis. It was the same kind of rampant global consumerism from

---

[3] No disrespect meant here for those who have pledged their allegiance to the defense and safety of their country and sacrificed themselves for this purpose. The commitment is huge and respected. But most of the 27 armed conflicts the US has been in since the Korean war have been about the safety and viability of our commerce and not our national borders. Also, with a professional army, a very small percentage of the population is actually involved in these conflicts which is why the fourth generation is largely untouched by the discipline and commitment of military involvement.

Shanghai to Chicago in the late '20s that led to that massive collapse. We're already seeing the early signs of it today (yeah, it's gonna get much worse).

In terms of relationships, we have to acknowledge that these historical influences have created an atmosphere where selfish behavior is the accepted norm. Getting the most money we can at work, dating the most attractive people at school, getting the best deal at the store... And we've now developed a language that goes along with all this:
• "What I'm looking for in a guy is..."
• "No, she wasn't really my type..."
• "I believe God has someone for me."
• "I'm looking for the one."

The one for who? You mean someone for you? It's a language of entitlement: "What I want, no, what I deserve!" This influence is subtle and deep, and like most cultural phenomena, everyone buys in. Based on this internal language, we come into places scanning, looking for people who will fit our criteria. We're looking for something, someone for *me*. Don't you think that's kinda weird?

If not, you probably feel like you're entitled to be loved. That you're worthy, "captivating", or at least that it would be nice if other people knew your love language and started to speak it just a little bit more... You may be approaching relationships with this core sense of rights. In fact, you may be approaching everything with a sense of entitlement:

Relationship with God
Here's a typical Christian worship song:
> **My** refuge and **my** strength, **my** comfort and **my** care
> **My** hope through all despair, You are a shield about **me**
> **My** rock and one sure friend, **my** light and only way
> **My** joy through times of pain, You are a shield about **me**

Relationship with family
In the US there are around 17,000 nursing homes "caring" for around 1.8 million of our parents or grandparents. It's around 7.4% of people aged 75 or older. This is the end of the long slow

deterioration of family relationships where my privacy and life is more important than caring for my parents.

Relationship with our work
The last ten years have revealed unprecedented greed and corruption in the workplace. I mean, how many yachts did those Enron guys really need? Somehow we've accepted the idea that we always need just a little more, so we don't work to create, we take. Jobs become a means to a material end, instead of a place of fulfillment and creativity.

Relationship with our creativity
The art historian Rookmaaker says: "For many [artists], art has become an individualistic search for their own identity through and in their work. They are like a person looking in the mirror; everything is an expression of self, and everything else becomes unreal."[4] We've moved from collaborative guilds to the studio of one. Bands go from No Doubt to Just Gwen (or the comeback of No Doubt when Just Gwen dries up...).

Relationship with that nice-looking guy over there
Dating has become a form of mutual extraction, or what a friend of mine calls "consumer relationships". We agree to take something, to try each other and see what it's like. We're not doing it for them, we're doing it for us, for our needs. When they dry up or don't meet our needs, we move on to the next target. It's why we date and fail, date again and fail again, and again... and then we're surprised when we get married and that doesn't work.

You can't get there from here.

So honestly, why do we pursue people. Is it for them or for us? You're attracted, fine. Is it platonic or is it loaded with your own needs? How do you know? Our needs run deep and subtly influence everything we do. We can so easily become co-dependent on God, or people, or work. We may stop taking risks

---

[4] H. R. Rookmaaker, *Art Needs No Justification*, Intervarsity Press, page 7. Rookmaaker was an art historian, scholar, professor, and author. He was particularly interested in the subject of artists and identity, and had a huge influence on Francis Schaeffer back in the late '40s at L'Abri in Switzerland.

after a while 'cause we get burned too many times. But if we know where we're at, and why, we can start to work on it. Going from a place of need to the ability to create love and give it away freely is what most of this book is about. If you can start with an honest assessment of your own selfishness, then it's not really that hard. In fact, the power of unconditional love is amazingly easy to grasp and understand; it's just hell to apply.

When 26 years ago I first met and started to spend time with my future wife, Heather, I learned really quickly that I had no idea what love and friendship was about. That was the first lesson. I was clueless and needy. But knowing that was huge. It prevented me from racing ahead with attractions, or trying to get her to marry my needs and calling it love. I took the time to process some of this stuff so that when I was with her, it was for her sake and not mine. During this time, I learned a lot of things that I'd like to unpack, but acknowledging my selfish approach to relationships was the first and most important step.

One way to put this on the table today is to break out your criteria. The lists we've been encouraged to form in our minds about what we want in another person. These lists detail the conditions of our love, or our "conditional love" (make that the title of your list). They clearly state to others, "I love me and this is how you can too". They're our expectations (which subtly turn into demands) of what we want others to be, and if there is one central lesson I've learned, it's that expectations sabotage relationships. But I suggest you break out your list and look at it. If it's in your mind, write it down, expose it.

This is really important for two reasons. One is that some things on your list contain values. We'll look at this later, but values are really important to hang on to when it comes to making commitments to people. Things like if you want a family or not, or how you treat money or caring for elderly parents... Secondly, your criteria reveal how your unmet needs translate into how you want others to fulfill you. This includes what you want them to look like, what their personality should be like, how they should treat you and take care of you. This exercise allows you to see how you've taken your need for love, provision, value and destiny and transposed it onto someone else. This is the root of destruction in a relationship. It's the beginning of a life of expectations, of "love languages" that you need fulfilled, and it'll never work.

How would you like it if someone came up to you and said, "I'm looking for someone who has long black hair, big brown eyes, a nice body, makes me laugh, and can cook Italian food really well". You'd be like, "Get lost, and take your list with you". But we do this in our minds all the time. Not the literal version, but the more subtle needs translated into criteria, and criteria translated into expectations. It's a waste of time, it's judgmental and it's cruel. Having things you like about other people is fine, but forming them into the image of your need is just wrong.

Finally, "I love me" is not a bad thing in itself. We can't love our neighbor unless we love ourselves. We can't communicate our heart and dreams without being really in touch with our identity. We can't commit to another person's set of values if we aren't clear about our own. But if we don't love others *with our self,* myopia sets in and we grow relationally blind. Selfishness runs deep; the heart is tricky. Staying 100% honest about how you're doing in these areas will keep your eyes open as you approach relationships and help you honestly communicate with people you're learning to love.

Practice:

At the end of each chapter, I'm going to suggest some practice points to think and talk about with those close to you. The idea is to change the *culture* of how we relate, at least with you and a few of your friends. If you want, you can do this by yourself, but it would be great if you guys were all on the same page together. Maybe the best approach for your learning style would be to read through the whole book and come back to the details. If you're disciplined, this would work well. However, if you know you'll never return to these points, then spend a few minutes right now to get the most out of the process.

- *Please take some time and do that 1- to-10 scale on selfishness; have an honest look at your relational motivations.*

- *Write down your criteria of what you are looking for in a person. Is it the kind of list you would want others to approach you with? What are the real values you hold and which ones are just selfish things you'd like from Santa?*

- *Consider your family situation, or some past relationships. How have you approached these in terms of loving yourself versus loving them? What have the results been like?*

- *Has a sense of entitlement crept into your vocabulary and lifestyle? And if so, how has this affected you?*

Two. Limerence

Oh, instincts are misleading
You shouldn't think what you're feeling
They don't tell you what you know you should want.
Death Cab for Cutie, "Lightness"

Being in love doesn't mean loving.
Fyodor Dostoyevsky, *The Brothers Karamazov*

Getting to the roots of our selfishness takes a mighty effort.
Everybody's playing the same game and it's so easy to go with
whatever makes you happy. But as time goes by, you find
yourself more alone, less fulfilled, and tired of the game. I say
hate the game and don't bother being a player. Work on the
important relationships in your life today (call your mom) and
develop goodness in your neighborhood (mow someone's lawn).
Because once you learn to manage selfishness, you can move on
to the next huge issue: attractions. You know how this works.
You meet someone and you really like them. You think about
them a lot and you feel different when you're around them. The
obsession is a little annoying and the awkwardness is kinda,
well, awkward. But it still feels good for some strange reason.
You tell yourself not to be so stupid, but continue to daydream
about the possibilities... So far, that's pretty normal, but what do
the attractions really *mean* and what should you do about them?

For now, nothing.

We're attracted to all kinds of people for all kinds of reasons.
Overall, it's a pretty great part of being human. But it's not a key
indicator. Seriously, write that on your hand or something. In
fact, I'm pretty sure you've already been attracted to someone in
the past and you acted on those feelings. How'd that turn out?
Or you may think the person you're attracted to now is "the
one", simply because you feel like it. Okay, but what do you do
in two years when you're married and then get attracted to
someone else (because it will happen). Does the new attraction
mean you made a mistake? When you lose attractions does that
mean the person is no longer valuable? Of course not. Like I
said, it's not an indicator, it's just an attraction.

Honestly, I think one of the reasons we lend so much weight to attractions is because we need something very powerful to pull us away from our other toys. We like our freedom and our flexibility. In order to give up some selfishness, we need someone to be so amazing that we'd be willing to trade one addiction for another. I don't say this to be mean; I'm just concerned about how important attractions have become in our decisions about relationships. A friend asked me recently, "How can you love someone you're not attracted to?" This is a pretty common question and it's really telling. We've gone so far down the rabbit hole, we don't know how confused we've gotten.

We really need to deal with some of the baggage we carry around with us, whether it's our social language ("he's hot") or our personal obsession with someone we can't even talk to. Next to "I love me", how we handle attractions is our biggest problem. And it's too bad, because they're a gift, but when we don't understand them or make good choices with them, they sink us.

So what do attractions mean?
If you take an evolutionary perspective, attractions are simply another chemical connection to advance the species. We're drawn to the fittest body to procreate with and we're away. In this case, strong attractions lead us to commit and have babies. But in the same way, if we're attracted to another person after we're married, our nature gives us the freedom to peruse that new person, because there's no moral imperative to the attraction. As in, "I no longer love you, it's over". I doubt that anyone actually thinks like this outside the lab, but a lot of people make terrible decisions based on post-marriage attractions.

I think the world has evolved, but I also see a beautiful design and purpose in humanity that comes from a Divine Creator. I think we're made in the image of God, which is where we get our emotional, physical, and chemical makeup. The reason we have attractions is because our faculties are wired to appreciate all of the incredible beauty in the universe. We're made to see, hear, smell, touch, taste, and consider all of this beauty, and to love it. Especially the diversity. For instance, there's not one kind of food, there are billions of combinations that you could create and appreciate. The same goes for music; endless possibilities just for the sake of it. In the same way, human diversity of body, personality, culture, and talent all make a near infinite beauty to appreciate. Attraction is the ability to see and feel and love this diversity. What an amazing gift.

So attractions are natural and wonderful, but do they *mean* anything? Is there an evolutionary or Godly design to them which we could use to develop relationships? I don't think so. There are some things in life which are there simply for the beauty of it, nothing more. You like some foods more than others, but it doesn't mean anything. If you add meaning to attractions, you will be confused in the long-term. If I just think of the last six months, I've met three or four incredible people who were super attractive physically, they had really interesting personalities, and I could easily spend all day every day with them. What does that mean? It means people are amazing, but they're not mine and I'm not theirs. Attraction is a way we appreciate people, but this will happen many times over in your lifetime. Does each attraction mean you're to go with that new person? No, 'cause all the attraction means is that you're attracted. Which is not to say that it's not great; it is, it's just not that important in making critical relationship decisions.

If you like a few people and you're really attracted to one of them, you could use that as a personal indicator and spend more time with them and build it into something wonderful. That's good. In this way you can use it in the mix of your overall discernment. But you should build that relationship on a lot of other things like shared values and mutual trust. Attractions alone are not an indicator. And you already know this, because I doubt that you make all your choices based on how you feel. At the same time, I still think we place attractions way too high in our list of values when we choose to pursue people or not. I could be wrong here, and would hate to diminish the wonder of attractions in your life, but at least let me caution you to not add special meaning to them, especially if you're young.

Some laws of attraction
I don't want to get too technical about this stuff, but here's a brief lesson on what goes on in our heads and hearts. Hopefully,

we might regain some sanity in the process. And I do mean sanity, because attractions can lead us into some crazy cycles.

Psychologists highlight a number of different causes for our attractions:
- physical attractiveness ("she's hot")
- propinquity (being around someone so much, you start to like them)
- familiarity (people you feel comfortable with)
- similarity (attitudes, interests...)
- complementarity ("you complete me")
- reciprocal liking (because someone likes you, you eventually return the favor)
- reinforcement (encouragement or positive actions you appreciate).

Some of this gets really detailed, like how we're drawn (or not) to facial geometry. Or how after being around someone for a long time, you suddenly see them differently, like, "Hey, I never realized how saucy your beard is, wanna get an organic smoothie?".

It's all pretty natural and you've probably experienced one or a few of these kinds of attractions. So far, you're normal. What may not be normal is the strength of the attraction and what you do about it. From the mid 1960s to the late '70s a professor at the University of Bridgeport named Dr. Dorothy Tennov interviewed hundreds of people to find out how they felt about relationships. Her studies have been continued by many others to further explore what she called Limerence. It's the intense feelings we have for other people before they even know us or reciprocate. It's the attachment we form before one really exists. Limerence is our preoccupation with another person. Attractions can be very powerful and lead to all kinds of behavior. In fact, certain feelings can become super dominant, so much so that the American Psychiatric Association is considering labeling Limerence as a disorder, similar to other OCDs (Obsessive-Compulsive Disorder).[5]

---

[5] *USA Today*, February 6, 2008. This is obviously the extreme version of attractions. I'm not trying to demonize them, but for a number of reasons, they sometimes get out of hand and become an obsession. When this happens, the smitten person needs to get some help.

Sometimes these feelings are strong because we simply like certain things about another person. Sometimes it's deeper; they might represent something we've lost or never had. In this way, they become a surrogate for unmet needs, like a girl looking for a father figure. This can get scary and you need to know if you're heading down that road. In either case (mild attraction or obsession), we're often not thinking straight, and so acting on the attraction too soon is rarely a good idea.

Loco en la Cabeza?
Even the more benign kinds of attractions can be loaded. For instance, what if you kinda like someone because you have similar interests (similarity), and you're hanging out together a lot (propinquity). Seems innocent, right? And it is. But over time, your chemicals kick in. Your body starts to release dopamine (heart rate increases—embarrassing!), phenylethylamine (this chemical is in chocolate, get my drift?), and oxytocin (creating a sense of bonding and trust—look out!). So even the sane amongst us start to interpret these neurotransmitters as significant signals of the heart or as a sign that God is "talkin' to ya". Umm, no. It's your chemicals. Which is not to say that it doesn't matter; it does. It's completely natural. You feel these ways because of real reasons. The strength of these feelings should be weighed though, and what you do with these reactions will determine the foundations of your relationship.

One of the first really dumb things we do with attractions is to talk about them. We grab our friends (or they grab us) and we verbalize the stuff in our hearts. This is a really bad idea. Nothing actually exists yet, but it's amazing how when you talk about attractions, they start to form a kind of relationship. Even if it's just in your head, it becomes an entity. Sometimes this happens when you really wish it wouldn't, like when "friends" talk about you spending time with somebody and they press you for the deal, when as far as you're concerned, there isn't anything going on. But once people start talking about it, it suddenly exists...

Timing
I think most people prematurely talk about and/or act on attractions. And once the cat's out of the bag, we race into relational cycles which are driven by the power of these

attractions. The first phase in the cycle "uninformed optimism" (feels like certainty). You start out thinking the person you like (for whatever reason) is really great. It's because you don't really know them yet, but it doesn't matter. Tennov also discovered "a remarkable ability to emphasize what is truly admirable and avoid dwelling on the negative". In this case, love seems blind. But since it's not really love yet, it's just blind. You start to spend more time with the person, thinking, "oh please, oh please". Remember what Santayana said? "Those who cannot remember the past are condemned to repeat it."

The second phase is "informed pessimism" (now it feels like doubt). After a while you get to know the person and they're not what you thought or wanted them to be. It's kinda unfair because maybe they never said they were that person. Instead, your needs created an image you wanted them to fulfill. The gloss starts to fade and you replace kindness with criticism. Most people check out of the relationship at this stage, which is too bad because you never get to the next stages ("hopeful realism" and "informed optimism"—we'll talk more about that in a later chapter).

Once the feelings wear off, we go looking elsewhere, usually hurting or being hurt in the process. Or worse, we stay connected in a weird way, dragging things out in hope, thinking the attraction means more than it really does. Why? All because of some chemicals? I'm not sure this is a good idea. In fact, for hundreds of people I know, it's been a disaster. At the same time, there are other people I know who have had similar attractions, but it's worked out fine, or not, but no damage along the way. So what's the diff'?

Ventilation
Being attracted to other people is completely natural, including same-sex attractions. The problem is not the attraction; what really matters is *how you think about it, what you say about it, and what you do with it.* Here's a few suggestions that may help you channel the attractions towards something good for both of you.

First, put the attraction in its place. It's not from God, it doesn't signify much, and other than being kinda nice, it's simply an emotion (or some fun chemicals). If it's really strong and it's hard to keep your heart in check, then get some help. But mostly, develop some self-control, 'cause it's a lost art. We talk about these feelings as though they dominate us and they're signs from above, when really we just like going for the ride. But knowing the ride usually ends in the sea should teach us to be in better control of our hearts.

Secondly, don't talk about them, even to your best friends (at least in the beginning). Maybe your dad if you can, because he's not gonna be sucker-punched by the idea. But otherwise, don't talk about it with people. Having said that, I really do think you need to ventilate your heart. I do this by talking to God. If I feel strongly about someone, I tell God what I think of them, how much I like them, and for what reasons. Doing this has two cool effects. One is that it relieves the pressure of having to say or do something stupid. The other is that it's like talking to *their father*. It purifies my communication and intentions. It leads to more respect and a deeper appreciation. Limerence can easily lead to obsessions, lust, or envy. It needs to be checked, and the best way I know how to do that is to expose my heart to God. So far, it's worked wonderfully, and I'll need to keep it up as I've been and will continue to be attracted to a lot of people.

Thirdly, you now have to decide what you will **DO** with the attraction. If you really wanna dance, you'd better be prepared to pay the piper. If you are ready to act on the attraction, then go for it. Tell the object of your affection exactly how you feel and be as poetic or romantic as you like. But you'd better be ready (*see Part Three*), and most of us simply aren't. In this case it's better to do other things with how you feel. For instance, you can encourage people, like, "I think that last song you wrote was really good, you should keep developing that talent" instead of "When you played that song, the moon hit your eyes in a certain way, that, well, I, I, I, well, I liked the song a lot...". See the difference? Of course you do, and you know when you're using encouragement to slip in the love vibes. Don't do it mister, not unless you've got that ring in your pocket.

You can spend time with people and develop a friendship without spilling your guts and blurting out, "I love you!", 'cause you don't yet. Instead, spend time developing your own life and future, so when you're ready to tell the person how you feel, you're also ready to do something about it because you actually *have a life* to back it up with.

I know all this sounds kinda sterile and way too contained. You may think I'm missing the magic and the wonder of an instant connection. But I'm looking for something better, and I've seen it. The bottom line here is that attractions are a natural precursor to a friendship. And friendship is much better than a pseudo "relationship". If you keep your head and don't rush into stuff with people who meet your criteria or those you're "instantly drawn to", what happens is that you start to see people differently. You develop a much wider group of friends, and you learn to really see them. And what you'll see is amazing. The layers unfold as you get to know people for who they really are. And not just how you want them to be for you. You'll see what's really true about them. *This* is attractive. And it's this deeper attraction which is so much richer, so much easier to talk about and love, that becomes the entry into a real friendship. And because it's not filled with the distractions of Limerence, you never have to lose it, or say you're sorry and drop the relationship altogether because you went too far too fast. Romance is based on commitment, and since you probably don't know that person well enough yet, just go with the friendship.

By the way—and this really pisses me off—I hate the way our attractions write off whole swaths of people we don't make time for because they're not interesting to us. We'll enter a room and head towards those we like for whatever reason, completely missing super amazing and wonderful people because we can't *see* them! Seriously, we're blind. And since we rarely take the time to find out just how beautiful, intelligent, and deep those other people are, we become more shallow ourselves. If you just want to follow the typical social or chemical patterns, then fine and Darwin love ya, but if you want to be human, keep your chemicals in your pants and start to look around the room differently. And find people who've suffered, or are typically marginalized, and spend time with them as well. It'll change your life.

Reverse Attractions
Another way to use attractions in a healthy way is to reverse the polarity. For instance, one of the common attractions is

"complementarity", which is when you add a missing puzzle piece to another person. So instead of looking for others to complete you, you complement them. I'm attracted to people I can help. When I see someone who needs what I have to give, I like responding to that need. I'm happy to fill a gap. I'm also attracted to people who are being marginalized and need "reinforcement". The ones who don't fit in. I relate well to this and want to add my affirmation to their diversity, or comfort to their pain. Maybe this meets a need of mine, in that I understand isolation. But helping others is the best way to meet your own needs. This builds on the natural attractions and strengths you have and, yes, chemicals will kick in. You will still have to watch your motives and communication, you'll have to pace yourself, but at least you're being proactive in a serving way rather than an extracting way.

The first time I saw Heather was on the deck of a ship in the South Pacific. There was a huge storm and nobody was out besides the two of us. She was wearing an ugly brown woolen hoodie which she'd tied down tight over her head leaving just a smooshed face which I could barely see. We said hi to each other. Neither of us were very attractive. Actually, I think we were kinda seasick. As time went on, we spent some time together in different situations. We opened up and she told me how much I was *not* like what she was looking for. Fortunately for me, she got to know me and didn't write me off just because I was not like the guys she'd read about in romance novels. I spent a lot of time with her walking through things I felt I could help with. Eventually we learned about each other's families, our histories, and it went from there. We used these deeper attractions to serve each other, not to be served.

I think Heather's gorgeous, but this has grown on me over the years. Not that she wasn't beautiful from the beginning, but the real depth of her beauty is a complex mix of her identity, her caring heart, her abilities, and her passion. You can't see all that in the first few months, or even years. I'll talk more about this when we look at friendship, but as we get to these deeper places in knowing each other, the pubescent-like emotions start to lose the power they hold over us. I'm talking about a relational freedom that creates a presence people will feel safe around, and that's really attractive.

So hopefully you're getting the message that our basic selfishness and our emphasis on primal attractions is not a good way to start a relationship. So what is, especially given that we're loaded with needs and chemicals triggered for all kinds of reasons? My suggestion is that we revolutionize how we relate. We need a radical departure from the typical way most of us try and fail at relationships. It'll take some time, but I think it's completely possible to change our orientation from conditional to unconditional love. It's kinda like growing up. You ready for that?

Practice:

• *What are you attracted to and why?* [6] *(Talk about it.)*

• *What attractions have you acted on and how did that work out?*

• *How has your communication of attractions helped or hurt you?*

• *If someone is attracted to you, how would you want them to treat you?*

• *Who are you leaving out because they "aren't your type"?*

• *What is deeply attractive about you and are you looking deep enough in others to see what's in them?*

---

[6] Heather, circa 1983

Three. Flow

Greater love has no one than this, that he lay down his life for his friends.
Jesus

Okay, here's the revolution. I think the best way to live is:
- loving yourself and knowing who you are (identity)
- developing something amazing with your life (creativity)
- consistently giving this amazingness away to other people (generosity)
- allowing the love you give to move through you, meeting your own needs (flow)

The power of unconditional love is this: As you love others for their sake, it creates this incredible flow through your own life. When you love, provide for, and encourage others, your needs for love, provision, and value are fulfilled. If people respond (which they mostly do), then that's icing on the cake, but the giving is adequate in itself.

For example, when you've been generous to someone, there's a feeling of contentment or goodness. It's nice if they thank you, but the giving in itself is enough. When you've served people with your abilities and helped them move forward, the fact they've done well makes you feel better about yourself and reinforces your own value. This is just scratching the surface, but I'm sure you get the picture. The idea is to make this a lifestyle which flows from a clear knowledge of your identity, and from your practical creativity being shared freely with others. Not as a doormat, but as a friend.

Going from a place of need to a life of giving is what maturity is all about. The best place to practice this growth is in the relationships right in front of you. Your family, your friends, and the people who'll enter your life in the near future. Here's how it works.

1. Prerequisites
Loving yourself and creating something interesting with your life is the domain of another book. But I really don't think we can

deeply love others and commit to them unless we know who we are (identity) and what we can make (creativity). We can start the learning process now, and a good friendship can help us develop our identity and creativity. But without a clear knowledge of self, we'll tend to leech off others to complete us. If you're pretty clear about identity, then read on. If not, please have a listen to this podcast as a basis for the rest of the process I'm about to outline. There are lots of other tools available[7], and by all means, get a better handle on who you are, but for now, this may help you start off:
http://www.patrickdodson.net/Podcast/Entries/
2006/3/25_Processing_Your_Future.html

Once you get a better grip on who you are, the next step is to develop your own creativity. I don't mean your artistry. Not everyone is an artist, but everyone's creative in some way and you need to know and develop your own creative strengths. What you make comes out of who you are, your passions, your abilities, your discipline, and the hard work of honing your craft. All this gives you the ability to share with others, and I can't stress how important it is to have something to give away.[8] If you're in sales, how can you develop your relational skills and develop a better client rapport? If you're in health care, how could you use your research skills to find new processes or treatments? If it's just a job, maybe you need to connect with your identity in a broader way and find work that's closer to who you are. Like I said, this is the subject of another book I have brewing in my head, but I think one of the reasons we become so relationally co-dependent is that we don't know what we have to

---

[7] You can look at StrengthsFinder, Myers-Briggs, and other tests to help fill in the gaps, but a really great place to start is by reading Robert Louis Stevenson's *On the Choice of a Profession*. It's fantastic and it's in the public domain so you can find it free online.

[8] Real love has to flow through who you are. If you're a chef, then love through cooking. If you're an actress, then love through the performance. If you're a nurturer, then show your love in that way. The idea is to be yourself and love people organically, along the lines of your identity. I do this by combining my love for food, hospitality, conversation, and interior design to create an environment that makes people feel comfortable, well fed, and rested. It's the combination of your abilities and motivations that creates the best ways to love others. It's when you open the channels of God's love (and God's concern for the poor, the disenfranchised, the unloved), that love starts to flow through your identity.

offer and so look to others for definition. So stay in school, or break out that good idea you've had for a while, and get ownership over your life.

Here's another podcast on creative development. It does focus on the artistic side, but I think a lot of the principles apply across the board:
http://www.patrickdodson.net/Podcast/Entries/
2008/12/19_Developing_Your_Creativity.html

2. The chronology of flow

It seems to me that growing up is about going from a position of constant need (input) to a place of consistent generosity (output). I think there are four basic stages in our lives that typify this development, and I'd like you to consider which stage you're in now.

Stage 1: input input input

As babies (including the really big ones playing WoW all day long) we constantly need input. If we don't get fed and touched and cleaned, we die. We depend *solely* on the love of others to survive. Babies eat constantly to become fat and cute, and that's okay, 'cause they're babies. But while babies are consuming, they're also observing, learning what love looks like. A newborn, for instance, can only see about 18 inches away, which happens to be the distance between their place on the breast and their mother's eyes. They're watching, learning, receiving.

Stage 2: learning to give

As children we still need input, but we start practicing some output. We imagine being a hero until our fort is attacked by pirates and we fall and hurt our knee. Then it's straight back to mom for some more input. We're developing our sense of self and our creativity at this stage. For instance, when a child says "no" to everything (called "the terrible two's"), what they're really saying is "yes" to being themselves. They're breaking the symbiotic link with their parents in order to start the output process. If their mom doesn't get it, and some don't, then the child gets punished or smothered. This will go on in cycles (at age 2, 7, puberty, marriage, midlife...) until a person establishes their sense of self and their place in the world around them (output).

Stage 3: real world practice

Teenagers are usually busy people. They're generally all about
the activity and they only eat to keep the engine running. They
wanna be adults so they're always out, trying really hard. They
may eat to make their mom happy, or ask for advice if they're
really desperate, but mostly it's about acting on the passion to be
themselves. The truth is, it takes a couple more decades to really
establish your identity, but to tell them that would just be harsh.
Young adults can be in a similar but slightly more developed
stage at college or the early years of work. It's mostly about what
you're doing or creating, and you get some input along the way.
You're testing your wings, and you make a lot of mistakes, but
it's all good because you're practicing, developing something
solid to share, like a new song or a new business. At this stage,
it's not unconditional output yet. People at this phase in life can
be the most selfish beings on the planet, delaying marriage and
other commitments because the circus is so fun. But the
opportunity is there to learn that it's more about output and less
about input.

Stage 4: output

The place of maturity is when you've settled into a good view of
self and you've learned to make stuff that you love giving away.
Whether it's as a great plumber, graphic designer, mom or
accountant, you know who you are and love what you make.
Your days are characterized by what you share, not what you
take. As you offer yourself to others, love is moving through you
towards them, and what goes through you (generosity, kindness,
intimacy...) meets your basic needs. You will be loved in return,
you'll have the provision you need, people will value you, and
you'll probably be very clear about where you're heading in the
future. This creates a sense of security and significance. With all
this going on, you don't have to take anything from anyone. At
some points, there will have to be steps of faith, because it takes
time for the fruit of this output to come back to you. Over time,
you'll become free and you will know that it really is better to
give than to receive.

*A little note here: You may feel like you've been in relationships
where all you were doing was giving and it didn't work out that
well. If so, I'm sorry about that. Now you have to decide if giving
is still a good idea or not. You may want to check if that giving*

*was loaded with an agenda, or if you opened yourself to abuse
because of unmet needs. In some cases though, unconditional
love is abused, and that's just painful, but it's still the right
approach.*

Can you identify where you are in the input-output process?
Sometimes we get stuck in a certain place, or even revert back a
stage. For instance, if a father does not take on a mentoring role
with his kids at puberty, the kids will find it really hard to break
through the input to output stage.[9] They stay stuck in a kind of
limbo, looking for a father figure to help release them into their
future. Actually, most of us just say "screw it" and head off on
our own, only to run into our own childishness later. I've heard
one psychologist say that the average American male doesn't
break emotional adolescence until the age of 27. And even at that
age, they can be spending half their lives outside of work on
some game (virtual, or real like sports, they're still games). Note
to the girls: Don't wait around for these young men to ask you
out, you .

Wherever you are in this input-output process, the place we're
trying to get to is one of consistent giving. Even in the midsts of
our own needs not being met. This is the beauty of unconditional
love: You don't have to be perfect or full to give it away. In fact,
the more you give love, the more your own basic needs are met.
For instance, let's review the four basic needs we have (from
Chapter One) and see how a centrifugal approach (love spinning
out from you) changes the whole game:

Our need for unconditional love
is met by choosing to love others *for their sake*
• *allowing a supernatural love to flow through you*

Our need for provision
is met by providing for others *for their benefit*
• *as you give, you multiply generosity 'nd this comes back to you*

---

[9] I've become convinced that dads need to take on a much bigger role when their
kids enter puberty. We've applied the Hebrew Bar/Bat Mitzvah rite of passage in
our family, and it's been amazing to see how the kids have developed in terms of
identity and an extroverted care for the world around them.

Our need for value
is met by encouraging and building up others
• *you can do this because you know the value of your own
identity, and if not, being an encouraging person has a way of
returning encouragement back to you*

Our need for a sense of destiny
is met by helping others develop their own potential
• *when you help others move forward, the efforts you make get
you moving too*

There are a lot of practical examples I could share, and we'll
look at those in later chapters. The pivotal point is that our needs
will only be met by loving others at least as much as we love
ourselves. The flow-through effect of this love will create
strength and grace. It makes us proactive instead of reactive.
We're not chasing after attractions, we're creating friendships,
which are the basis for the best kind of relationships.

Now, you could achieve all this with sheer will. I think the
principles work for anyone who applies their hearts and minds to
this kind of generosity. But for me, I needed help. As mentioned,
I had some baggage from my past, so I called on God to give me
a hand. I needed someone bigger than myself and my
experiences to help me learn the power of giving love. In fact,
when I started spending time with Heather and ran into my own
inadequacy (cluelessness as to how to develop a decent
friendship), I prayed specifically for wisdom. What I got in
response was God speaking to my heart, saying something like
this: "You have no idea what love is, and if you want, I can teach
you." And for the next three months, through some prayer,
meditation, study, and a lot of practice, I felt like God unfolded
the principles of unconditional love to me, or at least the
introduction.

I think one of the most powerful aspects of this journey was the
practical model of God's love for me. It was something clear and
simple, something I could replicate with others. The forgiveness,
patience, wisdom, and encouragement formed a solid foundation
for knowing what God was like, and a straightforward example I
could follow. I found healing for a lot of my issues by practicing
encouragement towards others, even when I felt like I was the

one in need. Change came through being patient in my frustration, forgiving those who had hurt me. I know this is in the bible, but these ideas can turn into religious hot air unless we practice these simple truths in the hard relationships around us.

As people of faith, we have these world-changing truths, but we rarely *do them*. I'm not sure about people of other faiths, but honestly, I can't think of one thing that sets the average Christian apart from anyone else when it comes to relationships. I'm not saying I expect more of Christians because we're better people, but we have this amazing opportunity to understand the power of unconditional love as modeled by Jesus, and we've barely touched it. In many Western nations I've been to, it seems that Christians date like everyone else and then break up like everyone else. And they divorce and have sex outside of marriage at the same rate as everyone else. One US study of people wearing "Chastity Rings" (a commitment to not have sex before marriage) found that over 88% had sex despite the ring.[10] Getting hyped about purity is not the same thing as applying the everyday commitments of unconditional love.

The Catalyst
So when I met Heather, God started working me on the principles. I just took this 100% seriously and dove into it. How could I approach her and not be self-seeking? How could I be truly kind and patient with her? Was it possible to not keep a record of wrongs, but always hope, protect, trust, and persevere with her? I got the principles, but I'd heard these things so often that they'd lost their power. Maybe it was all those crappy flannel-graphs in Sunday School, or the hundreds of hours of average sermons I'd endured... It's easy to become deaf to the power of Divine truths. I think the real problem is that we hear but don't apply, so after a while we think we've been there, done that, when really, we've never even started to touch the transformation of God's ways.

---

[10] Columbia University's Peter Bearman co-authored the most comprehensive study ever done on adolescent health and sexuality. Based on interviews with more than 20,000 young people who took virginity pledges, Bearman found that 88% of them broke their pledge and had sex before marriage. (quoted by Ed Bradley, *CBS News: 60 Minutes,* September 18, 2005.)

I wanted to walk in these truths, but my own background was raising its dysfunctional head. I needed something bigger than myself; I needed a catalyst. In a sense, meeting Heather was that catalyst, because it forced some issues in me. But I needed a special grace and enabling that would allow me to actually love unconditionally. God was providing the forgiveness, the affirmation, and the love I needed, and I truly *experienced* them for myself. So all the stuff was there, but I needed something to kick it into action. That thing was faith.

Faith has to be practiced; you need to do something with it to know the power of it. For instance, when God laid out principles in the *Torah* to alleviate poverty (gleanings, venture capital, crop rotation, etc.), there was a reminder: "Trust me in this, and you'll do fine." People needed faith to apply this stuff because up until then they'd never tried crop rotation. They didn't know about soil regeneration, or that generous giving to the poor would help the whole nation. The element of faith was that you had to do what God had explained and then you would see the power and wisdom behind it.

Catalysts kick processes into action. Like photosynthesis in plants. They have water and carbon dioxide as inputs, but they need *light* to catalyze the amazing process that creates carbohydrates (food) and oxygen (life). In my case, God had given me the basic inputs (love, forgiveness) and I needed faith to kick unconditional love into action by practicing a giving nature *before* I saw the fruit or benefit. I started by trying to be a really good friend. I practiced by learning to be an extraordinary listener and then becoming faithful with the little things, like showing up if I said I was going to... I branched out into as many different ways of showing love as I could, and with a wide range of people, not just focusing in on Heather. It didn't take long to see the fruit of this. People felt safe around me, shared their hearts with me, and just kinda wanted to be around me more.

I wasn't doing this because I felt complete or whole or empowered in any particular way. It's just that I took the idea at face value and practiced love, whether I felt like it or not. Cool thing is, the emotions followed, attractions followed and, most importantly, friendship. I wasn't trying to take things from people, so I got to know them, pretty deeply. After about six

months of this, I started to get really close to Heather and a
couple of other girls. It was a fantastic beginning and it started
the 26-year process that I'm unfolding here.

Flow
What I found after a while was that the self-sustaining vibe I got
from loving people became its own strength. It was such a great
thing that I stopped really caring about what I thought I needed
in the relationship. I think this is the main benefit of unconditional love: you get to a point of *flow*.

Mihaly Csikszentmihalyi coined the term after years of research
on what made people truly happy. As the former head of the
Department of Psychology at the University of Chicago and the
Department of Sociology and Anthropology at Lake Forest
College, he discovered that there is a point in our creative
endeavors where we are almost outside of ourselves. Through
mastery and focus tied to inner gifting and ability, people reach a
place of flow. Like a composer or an athlete who is so in the
zone of their ability, it's almost effortless. Another aspect of flow
for many is that the flow itself is the main reward. Money and
fame become less important as they reach this level of creativity.
Csikszentmihalyi, now a professor at Claremont Graduate
University in Southern California, has determined that there are a
number of aspects to flow:

- **sense of ecstasy** (like a runner hitting a certain distance)
- **inner clarity** (like a mathematician internally visualizing an
  amazing formula)
- **serenity** (the tranquility of being absorbed with your
  creativity)
- **timelessness** (being unconcerned with time)
- **intrinsic motivation** (creativity being its own reward)

He further describes flow as
> […] being completely involved in an activity for its own
> sake. The ego falls away. Time flies. Every action,
> movement, and thought follows inevitably from the

previous one, like playing jazz. Your whole being is
involved, and you're using your skills to the utmost. [11]

I've found that practicing unconditional love puts you in a very
similar relational state. The serenity, intrinsic motivation, and
timelessness are all part of a selfless approach to people. Since
you're not trying to extract something from other people, the
inner drive to take diminishes and you're free to be more patient
and kind... all of which is its own reward.

Living like this has been wonderful for the most part. But there
have been lots of times when I felt I didn't have the grace or
ability to care any more. Or that my past was catching up with
me and winning. There have been times when I've walked out on
people, unable to do one more day of this kind of sacrificial
caring. The dark side of need is always ready to pounce if it's not
kept at bay.

Last year I went through one of these really hard times, probably
the hardest in my life. It seemed like I just ran out of steam. I
know unconditional love is self-sustaining and that an agenda-
based love (acting loving just so you can get something from
others) is draining. I know that I'd been practicing the right kind
as best I could, but I still hit the wall. One late night I got super
depressed, felt like I was letting my family down and not being a
good father or husband. It wasn't for any particular reason, it was
just that I felt inadequate and that, among other things, the
rejection of my father was catching up with me again. I had no
grace and I broke down, cried for a couple of hours and decided
to leave so I didn't cause any real damage. I wrote notes to each
of my family, booked a ticket out of the country, and packed a
bag. By early morning, I had set out walking to the airport. I
figured the three hours it would have taken me to get there would
either strengthen my purpose or help me see another way.

About an hour down the road I paused at a bus stop. I sat there
going through the history of my life with Heather and the kids.

[11] For the whole WIRED interview see: http://www.wired.com/wired/archive/4.09/
czik_pr.html. You can also watch Mr. Csikszentmihalyi give an extraordinary
presentation at TED via this link:
http://www.ted.com/index.php/talks/mihaly_csikszentmihalyi_on_flow.html

My family was not the problem. They're wonderful (for the most part, but man, teenagers are sooo annoying), but I had no grace to carry on. After a while I started to remember that when I first chose Heather, when I chose to be a husband and father, I was in exactly the same place. I wasn't whole. I was angry with my father. I didn't feel like I had much to give. But I'd chosen God's ways over my dysfunction and knew my baggage would dissipate over time. And it did, but now I was facing the very same choice: walk away from the opportunity and responsibility of love (they always go together) and be alone, or dive into the fray and find a whole new level.

A choice.

I turned back and headed home. This has characterized much of my life. Not strong emotions that lead me (those were leading to the airport). Not a lot of wisdom or understanding or solutions. Just obeying the truth and learning as I go. So I walked back. It started raining almost immediately. I just got wet and kept walking. It wasn't a purifying rain, it was a heavy rain and it made me feel more depressed. I kept walking. I felt embarrassed and stupid and no better than I had been the night before, but each step towards home made a statement. I *will* choose others above my self, my need, my dysfunction. I will trust that God's ways are true if I stick to them, for decades. I got home (it was dark by now) and went to bed. The next day, I talked this over with my family and I continued the process: love my wife and kids the best I can with the creativity that's within me; press ahead each day and ask for grace to make good decisions; learn to listen well and put my energies in the right places... The grace returns slowly, and the flow returns slowly.

So yeah, it can take a lot of the time. Those who have entered the place of flow have put their 10,000 hours into the mastery. Love is like that. Unconditional love is not supernatural. It comes from God but we have to put it to work in very natural ways, like human kindness, patience, forgiveness... The grace and facility are there, waiting for whoever will take them on. It might not be easy, but the results are completely worth it.

Another little note here: Some say that if you are loving people in your own strength, you will tire and fail. But if it's in God's strength, it never will... That sort of language has become cliché and kinda unhelpful. I would say that God provides strength and wisdom, but we have to activate it, to incarnate it. It's very much our strength in play, and that's fine. I think the cliché comes from the idea that God wants to live through us, that we are nothing and God is all, we're just empty clones... Where'd that idea come from?

Practice:

• List five or ten identity statements (like "I am hospitable" or "I am a trainer") and consider how and with whom you could share more of that.

• Where are you at in the input-output scale, and what do you need to help you move forward?

• In what situations could you practice more unconditional love, and what in particular would be natural ways to do that?

• When you run out of grace for people, what's a good way for you to recharge?

• Have you entered the place of flow in other areas in your life (like in music or at work)? How can you extend that to your relationships?

Four. Love and Happiness

I have found that among its other benefits, giving liberates the soul of the giver.
Maya Angelo

Is it actually better to give than to receive? *Really*? Does bearing all things, believing all things, hoping all things, and enduring all things in a relationship make that a great relationship? Bottom line, will loving other people for *their* sake really make you happier? I mean, I'm basing my whole life on the idea that unconditional love is not only possible, it's actually better (happier, healthier...) than being self-centered. So this stuff had better be true.

Turns out that it is.

Over the last 20 years there's been a number of studies on happiness and well-being which show the benefits of giving over receiving. Harvard researcher Nancy Etcoff, a psychologist studying the emotional and biological sides of happiness, says in her TED 2009 presentation that "people are happiest when they're focused on loved ones [...], discovering, learning [...], not sitting in front of the mirror trying to figure themselves out". She goes on to say that the self-esteem movement has actually made it harder for people to be happy. She cites one study where suicide notes were compiled and analyzed, showing an extremely high recurrence of the first person singular ("I", "me", "my"). Her conclusion was that "self-focused attention brings mood down". In his classic *Paradise Lost*, Milton called this "A long day's dying",[12] the slow death when self becomes the center of the universe.

---

[12] Using this line as his title, Frederick Buechner wrote a novel in which all the characters "seem to be dying of is loneliness, emptiness, sterility, and such preoccupation with themselves and their own problems that they are unable to communicate with each other about anything that really matters to them." (Quoted in Buechner's autobiography, *The Sacred Journey*, page 98.)

In applying the rules of happiness to the raw material of most relationships (attractions), Etcoff reveals an interesting dimension to the biology of love. The brain activates neurotransmitters according to the attraction. *Lust* produces testosterone and estrogen, which is great for our sexuality, but not much help in taking out the trash. *Romance* produces dopamine, which feels great but is short-lived and affects only a small part of our brain. *Attachment,* on the other hand, produces oxytocin, which spreads over a huge part of our brain creating a sense of trust, well-being, and a long-term bond. I think we're wired for unconditional love, and not just for the propagation of the species, as Etcoff and others largely conclude. When we live selflessly, I think we also make a spiritual connection, one that connects us with the extroverted love of our Creator, allowing us to be *other-centered.*

In terms of money and resources, most people already understand that giving is better. But to prove the point, Harvard Business School professor Michael Norton has been running tests to see if people really felt happier spending money on others rather than on themselves.

> [...] the team questioned 16 employees in line for a company bonus of $3,000–$8,000. The team asked the subjects about their happiness before and six to eight weeks after the bonus, and how they spent the money. The size of the bonus did not determine how much happiness grew. Instead, the amount spent on others or given to charity was correlated with how much individuals' happiness levels had risen.
> The team also gave 46 volunteers either $5 (£2.50) or $20 to spend. They instructed the participants to spend the money on themselves or someone else. Again, the altruistic group reported feeling happier whatever the size of their gift.
> *The Guardian.* Friday 21 March, 2008.

This principle seems to work across the spectrum of giving. On the ultra-rich end we've seen Bill Gates team up with Warren Buffet to invest billions of dollars in international development

projects. At the other end of the scale, everyday people give
small amounts of money each week towards local projects like
Network for Good, KIVA, and YouthGive, as well as a zillion
other causes. It feels good don't it? We seemed to be wired
towards generosity.

In terms of personal gifting and creativity, teachers are *the* model
of generosity. Teachers are a classic example of giving
themselves for the benefit of others. It's well understood that
most teachers don't do it for the money, 'cause there ain't none
there. But some studies have even shown that merit-based pay
schemes (better performance = more money) were actually
counterproductive to the profession. In their studies, Ronald
Sylvia and Tony Hutchinson (University of Oklahoma) have
shown that teachers have an intrinsic altruistic motivation for
their work, the goal being to fulfill "higher order" needs like
"social relations, esteem, and actualization".[13] Their fulfillment
comes from engaging in and loving the community, which they
value over "'lower order" needs like security and financial
remuneration. I've also found this to be true with anyone who
knows exactly who they are and what they're good at; they
naturally want to share that abundance.

An interesting side note to these studies is the scope of the
giving. It seems like the more people you love, even in random
acts of kindness, the happier you are. This is true whether caring
for extended family or having a systemic effect on an African
nation. The more capacity and scope to give, the better the
reward. This is in direct contrast to the notion that one person
will "complete you". The stories we tell each other (in print or on
film) always seem to say that real fulfillment comes from finding
"the one". In the face of all kinds of evidence that it's better to
give to A LOT of people, we keep obsessing over the one, as

---

[13] "The study concluded that teacher motivation is based in the freedom to try
new ideas, achievement of appropriate responsibility levels, and intrinsic work
elements. The latter were of transcendent importance to our respondents. Based
upon our findings, schemes such as merit pay were predicted to be
counterproductive in service organizations which employ professionally trained
people." (Ronald D. Sylvia and Tony Hutchinson, *What Makes Ms. Johnson
Teach? A Study of Teacher Motivation*)

though that will make us happy. Strange, no? We're running in the opposite direction of the real party.

Renewing your generous self
So if giving is truly better than receiving, and in our heart of hearts we know that selflessness is really better, why the me-centric approach to dating and sexuality? I guess we don't really *believe* unconditional love is the best thing for us. Or perhaps it's because we feel like we have such a huge internal deficit, there's nothing much to share. If you look at the studies mentioned above, they reveal that family stakeholders, people about to get bonuses, Bill Gates ($$$), and gifted teachers all had something to share. And you don't?

Maybe this is where our faith needs to engage, enabling us to take steps to prove the reality that giving is better than receiving. But what does it take to kick this into gear? For some, it's a matter of choices. Doing what you know is right and being patient enough to see the benefits later. For others, it may be a matter of praying, "Help my unbelief", and then taking steps each day to reverse patterns and transform the spirit of your mind to create new habits. Pioneering American psychologist William James described this as the step-by-step, gradual movement towards lasting change. It consists of daily choices that amount to months of changed behavior, which will not only show the benefit of selfless love, but will make it a natural part of your life. Habitual kindness, natural generosity, and other forms of goodness will release all kinds of chemical kickbacks (dopamine, oxytocin, etc.), no prescription required.

For others though, a "conversion" may be necessary to rock the foundations of a long-term selfishness set in place for any number of reasons. Researchers William R. Miller and Janet C'de Baca have studied the effects of mystical epiphanies, revelations, and fantastic insights gained by people in extraordinary circumstances. The results of these encounters or radical interventions (which they call "quantum change") typically involve four hallmarks: they're vivid, surprising, benevolent, and enduring. Transformative turning points are well recognized in people like the Apostle Paul, Martin Luther, and Joan of Arc, but what Miller and C'de Baca point out is that this is still happening every day to people all around us. These "beams of light" often produce amazing effects like greater unity and transcendence, which the authors call "value shifts". Have a look at the value shifts they discovered through their New Mexico studies with men and women, especially the trend from self to something greater:[14]

Value shifts in men after a "quantum change":

From	To
• Wealth	• Spirituality
• Adventure	• Personal peace
• Achievement	• Family*
• **Pleasure**	• **God's will**
• Be respected	• Honesty
• Family	• Growth
• Fun	• Humility
• Self esteem	• **Faithfulness to others**
• **Freedom**	• Forgiveness
• Attractiveness	• Self Esteem*

---

[14] A write-up in the *American Journal of Psychiatry* summarized the findings as follows: "For some of the subjects, changes were much broader than for others, but in all what was changed was 'me,' the person's sense of self. Unlike many drug and some mystical and epileptiform experiences, the experiences reported by Miller and C'de Baca always convey a sense of the sacred and a sense of responsibility toward others and the world about them. Even if the subjects didn't believe in God (and two-fifths of them did not), they became more spiritual, less materialistic, and more compassionate toward others and themselves." (*AJP*, 159:1620-1621, September 2002.)

Women's value shifts:

From	**To**
• Family	• Growth
• **Independence**	• Self esteem
• Career	• Spirituality
• Fitting in	• Happiness*
• **Attractiveness**	• **Generosity**
• Knowledge	• Personal peace
• Self-control	• Honesty
• Be loved	• Forgiveness
• Happiness	• Health
• Wealth	• **Creativity**

Note: * means the value remained after the transformation[15]
[Bold emphasis is mine]

My experience with all this happened during a tragic time in our family's lives. My father had gone through a quadruple bypass heart operation in California and ended up in a coma due to blood clots moving into his brain. I was living thousands of miles away in Germany and was right in the middle of an intensive communication school. I got the call that he'd gone into a coma (he didn't tell us about the operation) and, without thinking, booked a ticket and was on a plane the next day. I guess that was my part; the rest was life and God. See, I'd been

[15] Dr William R. Miller and Dr Janet C'de Baca, *Quantum Change: When Epiphanies and Sudden Insights Transform Ordinary Lives,* New York: The Guilford Press, page 131. Check this book out. It's an amazing study of how spiritual and psychological influences create lasting change. http://www.amazon.com/gp/product/1572305053

estranged from him for years and we had only recently started communicating in a healthy way. Even still, my heart was ambiguous about him, what he meant to me, how I should feel... In fact, I'd grown very dry emotionally over the previous 15 years, due in part to this relationship. I felt he had taken my heart like an uncaring pirate, and was about to die and bury it at sea forever. Regardless, I knew now that I had to take some steps.

I couldn't get a cheap seat on the plane and ended up using all my miles to take the only place left, in First Class. It was an overnight flight but I couldn't sleep. What I could do was level that humongous seat into a flat position and drape that soft wooly blanket over me for the ride of my life. As I lay there, I started to recall all the significant memories of me and my dad. He was dying, but it was my life that flashed before me. As the past came into focus, some vivid truths resurged from recesses where they'd been hidden for decades. For instance, at age 13 when I was playing baseball, I could see myself looking around the stands at all the parents, wondering if he had shown up, which he never did. Or the many times I sat in some uniform (baseball, basketball, football) at the bus stop, alone, waiting for a stranger to take me to the game. Other sweet and sour memories came up too, like me with my mom getting milk shakes after a game, but still without him. It just went on and on and for the first time in years, I started to sob like a baby, uncontrollably, for hours. Not a cool thing to do in First Class, but all I can remember of the environment is an angelic flight attendant coming by from time to time and gently putting her hand on my head.

It didn't stop there. I ended up spending the next nine days at Mercy Hospital in Sacramento sitting at his bedside just talking, one comatose patient to another. I had no idea what he could hear or process, if anything at all, but the tears just kept on coming. I complained, apologized, read poetry, and went over our long history together while holding his still, surprisingly soft hand. As the staff continued putting various fluid foods and morphine into his system, I was going through my own cathartic cleansing. My brother came, and we finally watched my father take his last breath on the ninth day. We sang "Be Thou My Vision" as the Wind left him, and immediately turned from the room, walked down the long cold corridor arm in arm, crying even still.

In those few days, I processed 40 years of emotional, spiritual, and relational issues all compressed and suddenly expanded like an emergency airbag. I chose to love my dad even though it felt like I'd been beaten with something inside and then made to run continuous marathons. But walking away from the hospital, I felt light and open and a bit more free. I had loved him, and was loving him even more. The forgiveness, the apologies, the seemingly one-sided process had opened a channel, or rather a highway for God to connect that last mile between us. As you can imagine, it's had a massive effect on me as a father to my children, and continues to do so today. Quantum change: vivid, surprising, benevolent and enduring.

So whether it's a step-by-step renewal or the effect of a massive encounter, we need to test the benefits of a selfless lifestyle. In Psalm 34 King David encouraged us to "taste and see that the Lord is good". I agree. We should dive into this, in faith, which is based on the promise that God's ways are really amazing. But going into it, we need to know that honest steps must be taken to prove the matter. Choices to love rather than be loved. Maybe you've already had an encounter that's turned the basic course of your life away from being me-centric. But in an "entitled", "My Personal Jesus" type of world, there needs to be some step-by-step change to really establish the goodness of being good to others. The following chapters will highlight opportunities for this kind of walk.

Practice:

Remember, we don't give in order to receive; it's simply better to give.

• *What are some ways that you're naturally generous with your time or resources, and how has that rewarded you?*

• *What are some challenging situations (family? work?) in which it would be hard for you to show kindness? What kind of "baby steps" could you take in that direction? For instance, I had a terrible boss once who was constantly yelling commands at us (really, yelling). One day, after a challenge from God, I started*

*picking up my feet and RUNNING whenever he asked me to do
something. Embarrassing, but after two weeks of this, he drew
me aside, asked for forgiveness, and then asked me to help him
change his management style.*

• *If you've been focusing too much on a single relationship, how
can the two of you divert your efforts toward a larger group of
people who need your help in some way?*

• *Get some of the books mentioned or Google some of the
researchers I've talked about to get some depth in these issues;
I've just scratched the surface here. The reason I think this is
important is that we need to break out of our simplistic or
overly mystical approach to the truths of God. They lose their
power this way. If they are true, they'll bear themselves out in
ways that everyone should be able to understand. The hard
work done by these researchers deserves credit and gives us a
tangible expression of God's truth, revealed in neurology as
well as in Spirit.*

*Part 2: Working the details before
they work you...*

Chapter five is about understanding long-term
relationship cycles...

Chapters six through thirteen cover eight relational
killers/possibilities...

Five. I love *you*

The course of true love never did run smooth.
William Shakespeare, *A Midsummer Night's Dream*

When you get the foundations right (dealing with selfishness and attractions and building on unconditional love), you're ready to start the long process of deepening your relationships. The next eight chapters will look at the main tensions you'll face over the years of that development. It's not that I wanna focus on the negative stuff, but if we don't face the demons, they'll haunt and erode the whole affair. We also need to face our naivety about ourselves, our blind spots, and the subtle ways we undermine our own relational future. We have huge relational failure rates and yet do very little to actually change our *selves* as we move from relationship to relationship. How about we work on that?

By the way, feel free to get some comfort food to help you through the next few chapters. Or grab a good friend and take the beating together.

Ignorance is not bliss. Neither is the naive way we approach love: heart first, chemicals all in, and a selfish romantic narrative that keeps telling us this is going to be great, until it's not. When things break down, we blame the other guy and look for someone new, repeating the cycle with some other poor fool. This has become completely natural and what we've learned to expect. People talk about relationships like they're changing shampoo brands: "No, I'm not with Robert any more, I'm with Paul now." Our naivety is in the fact that we think this new relationship will work out even though we've never changed our own behavior. The word "naive" comes from the Latin "nativus", which means natural or native. So yeah, you're just being your caveman (or woman) self when you repeat these cycles. Party on, eh? And you do, only to find later (and sometimes that "later" has you wearing a ring on your finger) that tensions start to rise and all the chemicals disappear.

As discussed before, part of our naivety is expressed in the way we view attractions. We think the feelings or the chemical reactions are super important or something from above. Or we figure that if we feel it, it must be right. Or that since we've been praying for someone and this person is standing in front of us (propinquity), then they must be "the one". When we add romance novels or too many films to our perspectives, we lose sight of the important things. Like the fact that we don't really know the other person yet. So if we call it love, or even worse, love that *God has ordained*, then we'll think the relationship is invulnerable. So we dive in, thinking that true love or God will protect us, but it doesn't work that way. God can definitely help and bless a relationship, but the way that pans out depends on how we apply the truth about love.

One cure for naivety is a realistic look at what's about to happen and the time it takes to make things really solid. I've alluded to this once but will refer to it a few times because I want it to stick. The diagram below shows what I've found to be the typical relationship cycle (I mentioned the first two of the four phases earlier). The time span from meeting someone to reaching a point of commitment usually takes a couple of years (yeah, get used to that) and for very good reasons. So, let's say you've "met someone":

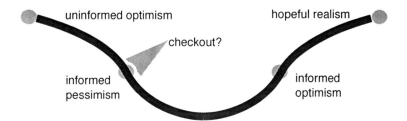

The first season: uninformed optimism
You think this is it, mostly because of the power of attractions (Limerence) or maybe because you need this to meet your needs. But it feels like love.

The ride is pretty sweet, so why slow it down with "pacing yourself". You ignore the warning signs and start a "relationship".

Really, the best thing you could do at this stage is to learn to be a good friend. Pace yourself, give them space and maintain your own. Be helpful without making them your life, or even a significant part of your life. Continue to work on knowing your own identity and values, without them at the center. Maybe you could encourage them to do the same, without trying to date or "save them".

The second season: informed pessimism
After a while, you start to really get to know the other person, and it's not what you thought, or more realistically, what you wanted them to be. You get a little cold.

Realism sinks into the relationship, but because you've already said more (or kissed more) than you should've, you feel kinda trapped.

This realistic picture is really quite helpful; it's who they really were all along, it's just that now you're not holding them to the fairy tale any more, because you can't. But it's all good, because now you actually know them, or know them better.

The problem is that at this point most people check out of the relationship. Especially if it was about meeting their own needs. Or if the attraction waned. Or if the other person didn't respond the way they wanted. Or if they just decided they wanted something else...

Sometimes you get attracted to someone else during your "checkout" phase and go right back to **uninformed optimism** with the new guy or girl. Stupid, isn't it? Go ahead and say it: "Hello, my name is _____, and I'm stupid."

My suggestion is to apologize for ever saying "I love you", "I like you", or "Let's start a relationship" when you really weren't ready to. But don't lose the friendship you have. And don't check out because they didn't match up to your expectations. Hold on through this phase, because you will be able to move to some place better called:

The third season: hopeful realism
Friendship is not based on being perfect around each other, it's when you really know someone and remain committed despite their faults. Hopeful realism is when you've had the time (at

least a year) to observe and partner with them in some meaningful way. When you understand someone to the point that you're completely realistic about who they are.

If you haven't been dumb enough to get physical with this person, you have the basis of a friendship that could last a lifetime, whether you get married to them or not. The goal of friendship isn't marriage. Allow yourself to go through the seasons without focusing on "is this the one"? Focus your relational strengths on building a world-class friendship.

If you have been physical with each other, it's a lot more complicated but not impossible to improve. I would just back off the physical stuff and focus on getting to know each other's families and histories and future dreams, beliefs... There are so many better things you could be doing than playing house (or doctor).

The fourth season: informed optimism
After a couple of years, you're not only realistic and hopeful, you're now confident about how to relate to this person. The confidence is based on all the time you've taken to observe and experience things together. Especially conflicts; wrestling with issues teaches you how you'll both react when the stakes get really high.

You've also had time to get your act together. You've finished school, or have developed your creative capacity so you actually have a life to offer instead of looking for someone to rescue you from your own boredom. You have a better sense of your own values and you've observed theirs.

If you've been really smart, you've never shared your attractions with them and you've never been physical with them, which means you've kept the focus on the friendship. This says to them (and to yourself) that you have a measure of self-control, which will really come in handy if you get married.

At this stage, you're actually ready to share attractions if you want to commit to them. And you've had history together so this wouldn't be weird. In fact, if you go through these seasons well together, sharing your attraction and your hope for commitment would be the most natural thing in the world.

Equally cool is that you may come to a point where you decide that even though you really love this person (in the best sense of the word), your real values and long-term priorities don't line up, so you'll remain as you are: committed friends. You can maintain this friendship for the rest of your life with no regrets because you haven't led them on. There may still be disappointments because you've spent a couple of years together and one of you may have been hoping for more than just the friendship. That's life, and it may hurt a lot. But if you haven't defrauded each other, the pain will be another milestone in a great friendship and will only add to it. If you have defrauded each other in some way, you'll need to apologize and be consistent from that point on. Learn to honor each other and never take something that doesn't belong to you. If you're truly unconditional in your love and they move on, you'll be able to release them in your heart, because you want what's best for them. It'll still hurt, but you will have loved them completely.

Heather and I met, developed a friendship around relief work in the South Pacific, traveled around NZ together, spent around six months apart, and then got married, all within a 16-month time span. A little short by my own standards, but the timing worked really well for both of us. I'm so glad we didn't date each other, rush into a quick commitment or spend time trying to act like we had a relationship. Instead, we *built* a relationship with friendship, a good sense of timing, and a lot of patience. I needed time to work through my crap, time to get to know who she was and where she came from, and she needed to do the same from her side. Two years is not a magic number, it's just that you need enough time to go through the important stages. The goal of these four seasons is to learn what friendship is all about. I think friendship is the highest relational value in the world. It is *the* model God's given us. It's the strongest relationship you can have. Even if you got married, you'd still want the whole thing to be based on and developed as a fantastic friendship. So start now, deal with the naivety, put your selfish approach behind you, and start working the real issues. It's worth every step of the process.

Practice:

Again, take your time with this stuff; maybe even pause here for a while.

• *Plot out past relationships and see how far you got in the four seasons discussed above.*

• *Think about some friendships you have going on now, where you are at with those, and what you are about to face. What's the next level you're heading to with them, and how long might that take, without rushing things? Can you cope with that?*

• *Do you have a sense of identity and clarity about your future? Do you know your values (the non-negotiable stuff, like what you want to do with your life, how many kids you want, whether you're an international or a local...) and do you know theirs?*

• *Are you ready to commit to someone forever, and if not, do they think you are? Why?*

Six. Commitment

...till death do us part,
or something else, we'll see...

The next eight chapters will focus on relational land-mines, issues that will blow up in our faces if we don't understand what they're about and how to defuse them. The flip side is that if we go into a relationship aware of these things, we can turn them into strengths. We don't grow in the absence of conflict and we can't run away from the potential of these problems. Instead, we can walk through them with perspective, wisdom, and grace, which is my goal in talking about them. The list below may be subjective, because relationships fail for all kinds of reasons, but from my experience and those of a lot of friends and acquaintances, these eight things keep popping up, so I think they're worth looking at. They are:
- Commitment
- Communication
- Needs
- Family
- Sex
- Money
- Abuse
- Everything at once

Then in each chapter we'll focus on:
- The problem (a breakdown of the issue so we can be more aware)
- The ways of God (principles of wisdom in dealing with the problem)
- The application (things I've learned in applying the wisdom)

We'll conclude each chapter with how these issues are applied to three phases of relationships:
- You're friends with someone and haven't taken things further
- You're getting really close to making a life-long commitment
- You're married

So that's the plan. Make sure you go through the **Practice** part of each chapter with some friends. We don't need more head knowledge about this stuff; we need action, and we need some friendly support to change how we relate.

The first issue: Commitment

A great friendship is synonymous with unconditional love. They're both based on a selfless commitment to the other person's well-being. But judging by the relational sorrow that's all around us, maintaining commitments has to be one of the hardest things on earth. So how can unconditional love give you the best possible chance to stay together? Let's start by looking at commitment first and seeing how the love of God, practically expressed through us and our choices, could possibly help.

*Another short note here: When I say "possibly help", I mean that God will not keep a relationship together. That's our job. Being people of faith doesn't guarantee that you'll stay married. In fact, I think the reason a lot of Christians end up in divorce is our naivety: we think that because we love God, we're gonna be okay. Not true. That has to translate into a very real and dedicated **commitment** to each other and the **ways** of God, not just a belief system that somehow keeps me safe. For me, knowing that I could totally mess this up keeps me aware of growing tensions, so I actually deal with problems before they get the better of me.*

I got married on August 24th, 1984. But it was a year and a half earlier that the process really got started, developing a friendship that might last 60 years or so. I'll come back to this kind of friendship later, but for now I want to talk about how unconditional love has held Heather and me together for the last 25 years. I mean, you think dating is complicated, or finding someone to marry is hard? No, that's the really easy stuff. Getting and staying married for a quarter century, dealing with a continual stream of issues to walk through and learn from and fight over, all the while dealing with money, children, work... that's the hard stuff. So hard that in most Western nations, around half of all marriages end in divorce. And by the way, as mentioned earlier, Christians in the West have the same divorce rate as non-Christians. So don't be naive; if you date and fail a number of times, what you're learning is how to break commitments. This becomes the pattern of dealing with conflict (leaving), so when you get married, nothing really changes.

The problem: I know this is repetitive, but I just want to say that most of us have lived our relational lives committed to No. 1. So when something is not making us happy, our commitment to self rises up and all the poetry leaves the room. Our promises fade and we start looking elsewhere for fulfillment. If I can generalize for a moment, I would add that this is more of a guy problem and less of a girl problem. As guys, we're often pretty relationally retarded, and very task-oriented, so for us, breaking a commitment can be like, "uh, how should I say... Yeah, more just like a change of priority, that's it. See, for me, it was never really a thang, you know, I wasn't thinking commitment anyway, at least not like she was. In fact, I'm kinda surprised she was so hurt. But it's okay, I'll get over my surprise". I hate to be so cruel to my kind, but you know what I'm talking about.

Another issue with commitments is the surprise factor. As in, "Surprise, I don't want to have children!" or "Surprise, I bought this car, you like it?" or "Surprise, we're taking care of my mother starting next week...". People start to crack under this kind of tension because they weren't prepared for the shift in priorities. This is usually because they raced into the relationship and never talked about the really important stuff (like deep-seated values). While dating, you don't really have mutual commitments, and what you once felt "completed you" is now tearing you apart.

Here's another biggie: being unfaithful. It's super destructive because it shows you can't be trusted, or that given a big temptation, you'll give in, which means you're not that committed. It's never worth it. Don't do it. You have self-control, use it. If you're really being tempted, it's because your life has nothing better to offer. Work on improving your life, your creativity, and keep loving others. Being unfaithful is about loving you; turn the tide on that and the temptation loses its power.

Note: Introducing this first section on the ways of God, I'd like to say again that this is not a religious book. Borrowing a line from Rabbi Sandy Sasso, "When we talk about spirituality, we talk about what we share... when we talk about religion, we talk about how we're different". These sections are about connecting spiritually to Divine Love, raising our sights to something bigger than ourselves to help transform us in our weak spots. If this is foreign to you, at least spend some time considering the points mentioned and apply them in a way that suits you. I've found that when I acknowledge my need and apply wisdom from God, I do really well. Have a go and see if it helps.

The ways of God: *Faithfulness, consistency, forgiveness, understanding, and mercy.* These attributes are mapped into our soul and psyche. They're not foreign to us. We see them in the natural world and sense them in the spiritual domain. Our conscience reminds us of them, our better stories inspire us towards them, and our world is crying out to see them in our time. It's simply a matter of application. The ways of God are designed to be simple enough for children to get, so how hard could this be?

It's really hard.[16] It's hard to stay committed when things get tense. It's so easy to cut people off or just leave. Especially when, as in my case, leaving is the model handed down to you. This is where I've sought help from God. What I've found by following God's ways has been super difficult but incredibly effective. What's astonishing to me is why we don't apply this stuff all the time, especially if we've known about God's ways for decades. But it seems to me, the more a person has been exposed to the truths of God, the more dull they become in these areas (unless they actually practice those truths).

I didn't grow up in church. I got taken every now and then by my aunt or good neighbors down the street, but God wasn't part of my life. When I did become a Christian at 20, it was like life went from B&W to Color LED. Each and every principle stood out against my lame way of living and I held on to them for dear life. I took this stuff really seriously and believed it could change my world. At the same time, I noticed those around me who'd grown up in church were becoming numb due to the repetition and the lack of modeling. Not everyone of course, but a lot of people I came across leaned more on beliefs than on faith and action. After a while our belief can become a set of rules and

---

[16] I've mentioned a number of times that unconditional love is easy to understand, but hard to apply. It flows when we allow it, but our selfishness will make it difficult to remain consistent.

guidelines that gets relegated to the sub-conscience. We know the talk, we don't have the walk. On top of this, a kind of weird subculture has formed around cheesy Christian art and music, insipid preaching, and chastity rings... Christian parents are getting divorced while our pastors are having affairs, all the while teaching about God's ways and how *we* should live. It's a story everyone knows, but very few live in its real dynamic. This has gotta screw with your head, right? So we start to discount a lot of this stuff as fairy tale and reject it, or worse, continue to believe it when nobody is really living it. So as I go through these basic tenets, please think twice about how you've actually applied faithfulness, consistency, forgiveness... Don't gloss over it all thinking, "oh yeah, I know about that". Instead, take a childlike approach and *do* something with it.

The application: I did *not* want to get married. I had a busted family background and a misguided sense of mission in life (like, dying for Jebus[17] in the jungles of Guatemala). Marriage was just gonna get in the way of all this traveling goodness (read: running away). So when I met Heather, it was no problem being "just friends". I didn't want to commit to anything that would hinder my flexibility. But deep down, I did want to know God and how things worked. So I asked, and God started working me, especially in the issues of real friendship and real love. A lot of it came down to making some hard choices. I understand more now about the idea that love is a choice. You don't make a commitment for what you get out of it. So I made a commitment to what Heather could get out of me. I chose her, not to be the one for me, but *to be something special for her.*

There have been many situations in our lives where we've had different views and priorities. Even though she's only two years older than me (but looks 20 years younger), we're from two different generations. She grew up in India as a mishkid (missionary's kid) listening to George Beverly Shea on vinyl (the guy that sang at Billy Graham's events), while I was in Northern Cali grooving to the Jackson 5. She walked hundreds of meters up and down the Himalayan foothills to go to school, while I

---

[17] "Jebus" is Homer Simpson's version of Jesus. It's the deity he calls on when he needs help, and the person he blames for society's ills. The usage sums up our weird thinking about God. Ahh, those Simpsons. Best TV ever!

drove my '74 Coupe de Ville wherever I damn well pleased. We have completely different ways of seeing the world. But we're committed to a core bunch of values that we established before we got married. Things like taking care of our parents if they needed us or how many kids we wanted, where we wanted to

live, what we wanted to do with our lives. Once these were on the table, we could make the overall commitments to each other and then deal with all the smaller stuff along the way. This is why a longish friendship is really important, to develop and articulate these things before you make any plans.

For me, the unconditional side of all this has come down to being faithful. It's something I become every day. When I stay engaged even though I feel like tuning out. When I use money properly instead of being impetuous. When I spend most of my time at home instead of finding amusements elsewhere to distract me. Staying faithful has been a struggle against my selfishness and my history. Everyone on my dad's side (and quite a few on my mom's) has been divorced. Right down to every one of my cousins on his side of the family. It's like a tidal wave of broken commitments that's deeply affected me. You could say, "shake it off", "you're a new creation in God" or "you're your own person now", but that's not how it works. When people in authority break commitments, they give your soul permission to do the same. Not to mention how easy the State and the Church make it to dissolve commitments. You can reject divorce in your mind, but that's not where decisions are really made when things get tough. In the real grind of life, it's the soul and the spirit of your mind that carries your true motives and therefore your final choices.[18] You have to realize that permission to leave resides

---

[18] The spirit of your mind is where your core motivations and experiences live. Your mind can house all kinds of ideas about the best way to live but, surprisingly, we don't often make decisions based on what we know. We make our choices based on deeper motivations and life experiences that create what the Bible calls "the spirit of our minds". Changing your mind is easy. Changing the spirit of your mind is a long-term renewal process.

there. So the power of being faithful, daily, is the counterbalance to the permission of leaving when it gets hard. Knowing how this works, and how deep the issues go, has given me understanding that I can actually do something with. I'm not *acting* like a Godly person, trying to stay married, I am *choosing* the ways of God daily, renewing the spirit of my mind daily, and that's turning the tide of generations. I am becoming faithful. After a long while, this becomes natural. Not that it won't be tested—it will—but the natural response will be commitment and faithfulness, because over a thousand good choices, you've been renewed.

That's the principle but, like I said earlier, we have to make this real by doing something with it. For me, this has come down to lots of little decisions and a few really big ones. The first really big one was getting married, diving in and learning to swim along the way. This is a commitment not only to a person, but to their whole family and history. It's like marrying a nation. This was really hard for me in the beginning, because the scope was huge, but over the years, it's changed my life. Extended family has taught me and covered me and prayed for me and challenged me to the extent that I'm convinced I would not be half the man I am without them. Heather's father taught me about heritage and a ton of other life lessons. Her siblings have supported and strengthened us over the years. You can't support a marriage between just two people; it really does take the whole family to make it work.

Another big commitment was to have children. I wanted none and Heather wanted seven or more. Again, I dove in and it's been amazing. Super hard, but the fruit is starting to show. We created an apprenticeship kinda thing with them where we develop their identity and strengths at an early age, which has resulted in them doing game design, directing film, creating art... all before they hit their 20s. I would never have been a part of this process if I went with my selfish intentions. For some of you, these kinds of commitments aren't where you're at. Thinking about this bigger picture can help you prepare. It'll also help you back off if you're moving too fast with someone you're not ready to walk this out with.

God's part in all this for me was the wisdom and revelation, the conviction when I was being stupid, and the hope when I thought I couldn't change. The blessing and fruit along the way also encouraged me to carry on. Which I really need, because that's just one of eight titans I'm facing.

So here's a few tips for applying commitment at different stages of relationships. Remember, we're talking about being more *faithful, consistent, forgiving, understanding, and merciful.*

1. You're just starting a friendship...
Start with how committed you are to your parents and siblings. How are you dealing with problems from the past? What can you be doing in your present situation that would *establish commitment as a model with those you're already connected with*? This way, as you further your friendships with others, you have something solid to offer. If you can't handle this with your family, it's naive to think you can do this with someone new. It would just be a matter of time before your roots started showing.

Faithfulness, consistency, and forgiveness should be the hallmark of your early friendship with someone. How are you treating them, respecting them, and caring for them today? Find ways to be consistent (like making your "yes" mean "yes") and be quick to forgive. This lays a really good foundation to build on, whether it gets any more serious or not. It shows people the kind of person you are (or want to be, even if you mess up along the way).

2. You're getting really close to making a commitment and have known them for a year or more
Now that you've had time to really get to know them, and they you, it's time to exercise some real understanding. Are you distancing yourself because you don't like something about them? Maybe you need to go deeper in friendship to really *get* them. If you find yourself backing out because of selfishness or fear, reconsider why. Remember, the relationship does not have to result in marriage. Just pace yourself and learn to push through difficult seasons, and stay honest about where you're at so you don't lead them on.

Intimacy is one of our greatest needs and yet very few
relationships in our lives are actually creating and maintaining it.
One problem is that we think intimacy comes from "the one" in
our lives. The truth is, intimacy comes from the community
around us, each person contributing different elements of
intimacy, like conversation, encouragement, physical touch, and
spiritual development. It's the combination that creates a
complete picture of intimacy. It's not top heavy, all loaded on
one person's shoulders. Most people at this stage of the
relationship are banking way too much on the other person
meeting their needs for intimacy, and it ain't gonna work. So
being understanding, committed, and forgiving will help you
balance out the load and let you build the friendship up. This will
keep you from being pressured into a make-or-break situation.

3. You're married
One of God's brilliant principles is to live in an *understanding*
way with your partner. God models this in how we are treated,
tolerated, and forgiven. One of the ways Heather and I have
applied this is to expose and reject any expectations of each
other.[19] Instead, we try to understand and accept each other in all
our various ideas and priorities. This acceptance has made a
massive difference to how we treat each other. But the real
benefit of acceptance has been this: the more I know of who she
really is, the more wonderful she is to me. So when it comes to
commitment, I have a rich perspective on who I'm actually
committed to: this real person, with all her amazingness, not a
loaded expectation of what I want her to be, which is no
commitment to her at all. This is the power of understanding:
that I get to see into her soul.

Understanding also enables us to see the long-term process we're
in so that we have the grace to endure when needed. Our
commitment is doable because it's based on reality, on who we

---

[19] There's a subtle difference between hope and expectation. I can hope Heather
becomes more savvy with paperwork (she hates dealing with bills and taxes,
etc.) and talk to her about it if I think it's helpful for her in the long run. But if I
expect this of her, my hope subtly becomes a demand for her to be and think and
act according to my values. There's a thin line here as hope turns into
expectation turns into demands. Even if they're good expectations, I have to be
careful, because I married who *she is*, not a clone to be filled with my values.

really are as people instead of what we're expected to be. There are no deal breakers, like "if you don't take out the trash, I'm leaving you". Instead, there's the long and steady process of growth that takes our hopes and desires and expresses them in terms we can live with. For instance, Heather would like it if I cleaned up after cooking. I think, "if I cook, someone else should clean up". If one of us held this as a deal-breaking expectation over the other, we'd be done. Instead, we have hopes that can be expressed through communication, sometimes in humor, sometimes in anger, but all based on commitment. When I communicate a hope, it doesn't have any claws attached. It expresses what I'd like and leaves it there. Ultimately, my hope should be about what's best for her. And the best way for her to arrive there is in her own time and way. Expectations are closer to demands. They're about what I want her to be *now*, for me.

Eventually, we'll work it out or find an equilibrium (like having the kids clean up), because our only true expectation of each other is to be committed. You may think this is an innocuous example, but when you add this to ten other things that could potentially annoy each other, this single little issue can become the last straw on the back of the relationship. Being committed to work out each one keeps them from stacking up on you.

Practice:

- *In which ways has commitment been modeled to you, and is that baggage or a blessing?*

- *As a result, do you fear long-term commitments or look forward to diving in?*

- *Do other people see you as a faithful person, a consistent person?*

- *How are you showing your commitment to the people in your life already? This is the foundation for your future relationships, so how's it going?*

- *Are the principles of God, like faithfulness, meaningless to you or an active part of your life?*

Seven. Communication

Marge: *Homer, I really don't like you telling personal secrets in your class.*
Homer: *Marge, I didn't tell 'em personal stuff.*
Marge: *Today at the Kwik-E-Mart everybody knew I dyed my hair!*
Homer: *Oh, you mean about you.*
Greg Daniels (episode writer), *The Simpsons*, "Secrets of a Successful Marriage"

Over the years, I've studied and received tons of good advice on communication. I've also studied marketing and run numerous courses and workshops on the subject. In general, I'm a pretty good communicator, but if you push my buttons, or things get tense, I'll revert to my instincts and all that knowledge disappears. When things get really hard I'll shut down, go into my head, and find some angle of defense or respond in an intellectual way—and that's only if I haven't found the door first. You may not act like this in the beginning of the relationship, when you're putting your best foot forward. We have our "best-self response" at this stage. But over time you communicate from the spirit of your mind, the stripped-down raw stuff that exposes our true motivations and needs when we're unguarded. This needs some renewing.

The problem: Relationships are a form of communing with another person. Connecting deeply, visually, physically, spiritually, verbally. The root of the word "communicate" is "commune" (from a Latin root meaning "to share or have in common"). This kind of deep connecting is the basis of intimacy, which is wonderful. But it also opens people up to their deeper, darker side and all the lovely buttons therein. As you get closer to someone, you move from shallow conversations to real hopes and concerns. You open yourself up as the communication gets richer. The more open, the more vulnerable. Your guard drops, allowing you to respond from the heart. This kind of openness is great, even if your worst side comes out. But all this has to happen in an accepting environment, or things will go wrong.

For instance, a few years ago I was going through a really hard season. It seemed a number of things all came down at once. During this time Heather and I were arguing over something really stupid, but something inside me snapped. I shut down and couldn't talk to her for over seven months. Yeah, seven months. We only communicated the bare minimum. She wasn't the problem; it was me and my limited capacity to deal with all the stuff that had built up. It drove her crazy and me into a spiral. I shared with friends and got some counseling, but it didn't break the back of the issue. I needed something deeper.

The ways of God: *God is a communicator, intimate (open), wise, encouraging, exhorting, just.* I knew these things in principle, but I needed to incarnate them. I had been praying and trying my best to apply this stuff. I didn't leave and neither did Heather (I think we have the commitment thing down, so far). But I couldn't find a way to work through the stuff that had built up, and I couldn't talk about it. One day, I took a long drive and sat on the beach, knowing I had to settle this thing. It was my birthday, and I'd been fasting all week to find some wisdom and grace. The day was sunny and long, so I sat there for hours, hungry, tired, beaten. I meditated on the last six months, the last few years, my dad, my kids. I knew what I needed to do, what I should say, but I needed something supernatural to overcome my inability (or stubbornness, who knows?). The conversation went something like this:

Me, all day long: "I don't have the strength to live down my past and be something else. I should just disappear."
God: "Wherever you go, nothing will change. You have to take YOU with you."
Me, all day long: "At least I won't be damaging my family with my crap."
God: "They can take it; they have so far."
Me, all day long: "I need some healing, or wisdom, or something, I don't even know."
God: "What you need is to be with them. That's where the grace is. It's not on this beach."

The application: So I get up, head to my car, drive back home, and start the long slow process of more openness, encouragement, servanthood. God was right. The solution was in choosing communication, not silence. It was by re-engaging despite my need and baggage. The result was more depth, more acceptance, and more pain. It was not going to be easy, but have you ever noticed the presence and beauty of people who've suffered? People don't grow or change in the absence of conflict. Change happens when we face the things that we would rather avoid, when we have the conversations we don't want to have. What I learned through this is that the power of God is not in some magical change of heart, as in "make me more like you". The power is in the hard choices to talk it out regardless. That's where you find the real grace and wisdom.

Note: The room that Heather gave me during this time was amazing on her part. On my side, I really needed it. A lot of people would have freaked out on me and either left or tried to force the issue. It would have blown up on us. Giving people space is really important. Let them decide when they're ready to talk. If they have to contend with you, they can't focus on their internal issues.

I don't know if this is harder for guys in general, or if it's just personality types, but I don't like talking about the hard stuff. Heather, on the other hand, wants to go as deep as necessary and bring the conversation to completion. Neither of us needs to change our styles if that's all it is, but as guys I think we have to own the fact that we often check out, not as a personality trait, but as a character flaw. In this way, our failure to communicate can also be a form of abuse. Most young men these days seem to have been raised by women, and not by their fathers. What I've seen is that men often react to the absence of fathering with bitterness and disappointment, and they take it out on those closest to them: their moms, and then women in general. I think the mean-spirited, uncommunicative way men generally treat women is a form of payback. This subtle influence works its way towards more aggressive behavior and can get really ugly. Therefore, I think it's imperative, particularly for us as guys, to learn to talk about the hard stuff, so we can get all this on the table instead of perpetuating the communication abuse we've become known for. The power of God will unfold when we make the choice to go there. If we don't, we will repeat the sins of our fathers.

So the application is to imitate the ways of God (open, honest, caring, listening, encouraging, enduring, patient). I once color-coded the biblical book of Proverbs into various topics. In doing so, I noticed there were tons of scriptures on communication. Like, "a gentle answer turns away wrath" and "good news from a far away land is like water to the soul". It was all over the place. The wisdom was out there, it was just a matter of learning those things and making them my own through lots of daily choices. Not complicated, not rocket science, degrees aren't necessary for this; just apply the stuff you know, like children. So let's look at how this works in the three stages set out in the previous chapter:

1. You're just starting a friendship...
Why talk of love when you can encourage someone? Really, trying to act like a grown-up when you're 19 is kinda pubescent. Let it go. You're not ready or able to love someone at that stage, so do something way better: encourage them. Don't talk about how you feel, talk about how you see them. And not just their hair or musical tastes, but what you see in their identity, their potential. The root of the word "encourage" is the Latin "cor", or heart. When you really encourage someone, you give them heart, courage. This is a far better way to communicate than to wax lyrical about the range of emotions you think are important right now. If you want to be really open, share about your history or your family or your hopes and dreams for the future. Talk about the really important stuff so they can get to know you. And be a world-class listener; it's the other half of communication. Learn to take time, to really hear and process what the other person is talking about. That's what friends do, and friends is all you are at this stage.

2. You're getting really close to making a commitment and have known them for a year or more
At this point you're ready to learn what my friend Matt Rawlins taught me. There are two kinds of communication: controlling and committed.
Controlling communication is:
• when you have agendas hooked into what you say
• when you try to keep the conversation from getting emotional
• when you withhold certain things to keep the conversation on your track

e.g. You feel you're ready to make a commitment, but you're waiting for a sign or something from the other person, so you don't talk about where you're at. You don't want to risk it (withholding information). Or when things get serious, you shift the conversation to avoid the issue (controlling the agenda). These are forms of control.

Committed communication is:
• when there's no agenda in the communication, you're free to go wherever the conversation leads
• when you may not like things getting emotional, but you don't try to shut it down if it heads that way
• when you share all the information and let the other person do what they want with it

e.g. Instead of waiting for a sign, you share how you feel, open to the fact that it may not be reciprocated. You're committed to honesty. Or, instead of herding the conversation away from the important stuff, you go there because you want things on the table. You're committed to hearing their side and don't shy away from what they want to talk about.

In both of these latter examples, timing is a scary thing. If you're
• spending a lot of time with someone
• and you really like them
• and you feel you know enough about them (and their past, family, etc.)
• and you're clear about your own identity and values...

...then you're probably ready to talk about commitment. But how do you know if they are?

Two things: firstly, if you have known them for a year or two, you'll have a pretty good idea of where they're at with this question. Secondly, committed communication means if you're ready but unsure, you ask them. Don't try to *control* their response by not saying anything, or using innuendo to subtly draw it out of them. If you want honesty and openness to be a hallmark of your relationship, start here. They may not be ready, but they should tell you that, and if you have a great friendship, you can bear it.

Note to the girls: Waiting for guys to initiate this kind of communication is kinda crazy. I know it's a cultural value, but it's pretty unrealistic. Most guys are behind the curve when it comes to relational commitments. They're often also task-oriented, so their head isn't usually in the game. You, on the other hand, are more likely to be wired with strengths like intuition and timing. You may misuse the gift if your need has superseded the friendship, leading you to jump in too soon, wanting to know if the guy likes you, wanting him to save you. If you're sensing that internal need, don't act on it. Use the strength you have and get a sense for the timing of commitment. Then, if he's not talking about it, maybe you should, because you're probably right. If you think God's idea is that the man leads the relationship, think again.. You may be missing your chance to teach guys how all this works.

On another note, there's a really good book my nephew is going through right now called *101 Questions to Ask Before You Get Engaged*. The first chapter is entitled "Never Marry or Get Engaged to a Stranger". The book proceeds to ask a ton of really good questions to help you really get to know the person you're thinking of committing to. For instance, question 54: "How comfortable are you with confrontation or conflict? How do you usually resolve conflicts?" The questions go deeper as the book goes on, making you look at issues you may not have thought about. I would highly recommend reading this so that you get used to talking about the tough stuff. It's a little religious and even cheesy at times, but overall it's got some good stuff in it.

This brings up another aspect of communication: pace. When Heather and I first started hanging out together, we mostly talked about things we wanted to do in the future. Later, it was stuff about our families, and then things closer to our hearts. After more time, we started talking about how we felt and what it would be like to be together. A lot of people reverse this process. Not a good idea. Pace yourself in your communication. Leave room for people to slowly unfold, and don't talk about issues of the heart unless your heart and mind and soul are ready to commit to that person for the rest of your life. Really, don't play around with emotional communication unless you can back it up.

3. You're married

In the first few years of our marriage, we learned fast that you cannot communicate your expectations or how you want your partner to be towards you. Real love is when you see them and appreciate them for who they are, especially their diversity. It's how you see the real beauty in the layers of their personality and spirit and gifting. This wasn't easy to get to. Our needs create expectations that "she should love me the way I want to be loved". I think this is called "love languages" and I also think it's a trap. The language of love is acceptance, not expectation. Being sensitive to what the other person likes is fine, but there's some quicksand here.

If you express what you appreciate (gifts, touch, encouragement) to another person, the heart can subtly weave this communication into expectations. This, along with the spirit of entitlement, creates a slowly growing burden over time. It seems noble in the beginning, that you really love them because you're willing to do something that's unnatural to you. Um, no. You now have to move away from your organic way of loving and spend the rest of your days trying to be something else for them. So on one side, love languages strengthen selfishness on the part of the receiver, and on the other, they turn the giver into a pawn. Hard words? Does it seem loving to acknowledge the desires of others and respond to them? How could that be wrong, right? I know, the concept of love languages has been wrapped into the psyche of our culture and made to look sacrificial and good, but it's tricky. If you want to be loving, and maintain that love, it has to come from your heart, from who you are (your preferences, your identity) in an unconditional expression of your *self*. You can try to love someone the way they want, but you probably can't sustain it forever. And they shouldn't be holding out waiting to be loved in a certain way either; it just pushes all those selfish buttons.

If they like chocolate, go ahead and give it to them (especially that 70% cocoa, Fair Trade goodness). That's called being sensitive and kind. But love languages play hard on our sense of entitlement, so you really have to be careful. And it's lame to tell people what you want for Christmas; let them love you the way they want, because then it's genuine and unique. For me and Heather, this means we can say what we like, what we appreciate, and leave it there. But where we really communicate our love to each other is in the acceptance of our differences, and in the slow, wonderful unfolding of our hugely diverse personalities. We communicate love through encouragement, healthy arguments, and acts of kindness that come from our hearts, not the other person's wish list. You may be able to sustain the "love language" gig for a few years, but if you wanna be in this for the long haul, you may want to consider what I'm saying.

Note: I mentioned we love each other in arguments. We've learned to fight well by being open and honest, passionate but also good listeners. But the real strength of fighting well comes from the solid basis of commitment. In other words, regardless of this argument, or disagreement, or playful scuffle, I am not changing my commitment to her as a person. If that's true, we can talk about anything, and should.

One area I have to be sensitive with is non-verbal communication. I can be in my own space a lot of the time, and this sends a "distance" message. I'm not trying to say I don't need people around, I'm just in my own head, but that is telling people something. So I have to be aware of what I'm saying non-verbally, and need feedback from others to know this is happening. Then I can compensate for it by being more verbal, reinforcing how I really think and feel about those around me. I still need to be me, but I also need to be sensitive to how this is affecting my family.

Finally, there are lots of things we do as a family to communicate our love in a formal way. I think it's kind of a lost art, like family traditions in general, which have been supplanted by YouTube (or any tube). If txt, Twitter, FaceSpace or whatever has created a fragmented home, then you need to counterbalance the inputs. One way we do this in my family is through bar or bat mitzvahs. We have a formal ceremony when our kids turn 13, and we acknowledge them. We speak out encouragement and celebrate who they are at birthdays and other special events. This is another book in itself, but I just want to point out that through these intentional encouragements, formal communion times, and a few other things, we are remembering what's important and making sure we *say it* so it sticks.

Practice:

• *In terms of your communication, what are your strengths and weaknesses (open? honest? verbal? non-verbal? controlling? committed?)?*

• *When you're with your family, how do you communicate (or not)? And how is this different from when you're with your friends or "significant others"? Why is it different, and is it possible you're only acting with your friends? When they really get to know you, will you revert?*

• *How could you formalize certain events (birthdays, a new job or graduation) to make things special or memorable?*

• *How do you communicate love naturally?*

• *When other people love you in a way that's natural for them, do you acknowledge it, or ask for something else instead?*

note: This is where Maxwell got his Fro ideas from.

Eight. Needs

Love, love me do.
You know I love you,
I'll always be true,
So please, love me do.
Whoa, love me do.
The Beatles, 1962 (timeless eh? our needs, that is)

We've already talked about how we have huge needs and
selfishly try to get them met in relationships, which usually ends
up killing the relationship. But in saying that, I want to stress that
those needs aren't wrong; it's how we meet them that messes
things up. We need love, provision, value, and a sense of destiny.
That's all good. But if we look to another person to fulfill those
needs, we'll suck them dry or end up pushing them away. No one
person can be all these things to you. In fact, the only way to
have these needs met is to give the very thing you want to those
you choose to love.

This is probably the biggest paradox of relationships. You give in
order to receive. Even in your need, you give. If you need
encouragement, you give it. If you need some provision, you
share or even sacrifice what you have to help others. This simple
paradox has saved my relational life. The power of love is in the
giving. It's a kind of internal strength and grace that quenches
the desperation. I haven't found anything as sustaining and
beautifully simple as the love I give to others.

The problem: When I bring my unmet needs into the
relationship, it subtly poisons everything. Innuendo seeps into
the communication ("So why didn't you call?") and tensions
easily rise over very small things ("You bought what?"). I can
make it sound like I'm concerned about our money, but if my
core nervousness comes from a lack of provision in my life, or
knowing how it works, then I'll take it out on those closest to
me. Here are some ways it can pan out:

Our need for unconditional love becomes: an unbalanced sex life
(a struggle to understand intimacy), a constant need for attention,
doormat behavior, demanding behavior, co-dependency...

Our need for provision becomes: nervousness, insecurity, poor stewardship, time management issues, misguided faith (like, "God will provide" when it's not really the issue), money problems...

Our need for value becomes: low self image, discouragement, joblessness or constant job changes, neediness, openness to abuse, co-dependency...

Our need for destiny (a clear sense of our future and purpose) becomes: co-dependency on other people's future, mid-life crisis, disconnected fantasies, workaholism...

All these unmet needs start to act like a cancer in the relationship, like good cells gone bad. If we entered relationships to create and give, these needs wouldn't undermine the process, but if we are "looking for love", we're screwed.

The ways of God: *Servant, facilitator, healer, teacher, provider, encourager.* Again, I'm trying to track how God treats me in these ways so I can do the same for the people in my life. In fact, one of the life lessons I've developed over the years has come directly from the way God has met my need for value (encouraging me, reminding me what's important). In hearing this pretty regularly, I have a good sense of identity and how that plays out in my creativity, provision, and even my life's calling. As God has encouraged me, loved me despite my ignorance and arrogance, and provided for me, I have something to give to Heather, my family, and my friends.

The application: Unconditional love was the biggest unmet need I brought into my relationship with Heather. With my family background and a very young faith, I could have easily swamped her with my needs and stretched her beyond capacity. In fact, any love that's *required* only begets contrived responses. So I determined right in the beginning to love her the way I was being loved by God.

This may sound noble or even big-headed, but it's not. What I did was simple and straightforward. It wasn't hugely spiritual or gallant. It was just a matter of consistently choosing for her best, using what I had to give. I loved her, not me. I loved her in ways that I was capable of and that were natural to me. I didn't try to perform for her or meet her expectations (as if I could). I just loved her. I encouraged her. I made space for her and gave her my time. I cooked for (and with) her. I listened to her history and values. I wrote to her family to get to know them and allow them to get to know me. I made her the priority. I chose to meet her needs where I could, and where I couldn't, I was a friend and partner.

In summary, I wasn't focusing on my unmet needs; I was fulfilling hers in ways I was able to. This isn't martyrdom, it's just outward-looking. Instead of concentrating on what I wanted, I spent my abilities on someone else. It made all the difference. I don't do this all the time, but it's not because I'm unable to. As I've reiterated before, love like this is actually self-sustaining. The reason I sometimes don't is because I'm selfish, and that gets the better of me at times. For example, when we started to get serious with each other we started to share our values, and one of those was how many children we wanted. I mentioned earlier that she wanted a lot and I didn't (read: zero). I thought my need was for space and peace, two things children eat up and pooh out. I actually thought this zero kids thing was a value that shouldn't be compromised. In reality, it was another form of me running, and I wanted to drag Heather with me.

After thinking about it for a while, I could see that Heather was going to be an extraordinary mom. My question became: Am I a father? People had spoken to me about this, about how I was a chief and father and leader. I never really related to this because I was still looking for provision and value. I was translating my unmet need for a father into other weird things that no one could fulfill. Had I dragged that need into this question, I would still be single today, or at least without Heather. Not that being single is wrong, but being selfish will always lead to being alone. So instead, I chose to *be* a father. I went with Heather's values because mine were busted (at least in this area), and deep down, I believed the words spoken over me, that I actually was capable of being a good father. I made choices and commitments and voilà, I'm now one of the world's best dads, I don't care what my kids say (and they'll say anything for some easy tabloid cash).

Okay, so how do you cope with unmet needs in the three stages:

1. You're just starting a friendship...
This is a great place in a relationship to be honest about your past and your needs. Get real with each other before things get loaded or you start "need-dating". You may think that if you're honest about who you are and where you've come from, people will reject you. Some will—better now than later. But the ones who hold on to you are worth their weight in gold. If you can be open at this foundational stage, then you can work through anything as time goes on.

When Heather and I met, we were on a course where issues came up all the time. Half of our conversations were about stuff we were working through, so we had this really open basis to build on. When it came to meeting needs, it became easy to see when someone was trying to work the other person, to have them be a surrogate for the issue they wanted to escape.

Acknowledging this allowed us to either back off or learn to help each other if we could. I tried to practice this with the group of friends I was with at the time (around 15 people). I made it a kind of project to meet the needs of others instead of my own. The response was pretty great. People were nicer to me, respectful, and often returned the kindness. Not that that's the goal, but it's a nice value added.

2. You're getting really close...
At this stage you have to do some hard-core self-analysis (or get a pro to do it with you). You have to go deep into your heart to check the motivations. Are you entering this relationship for what you can get out of it? If you are, it'll grow from an innocent need ("I'd love someone to cook for me") to a monstrous demand ("Why aren't you taking care of me?"). How many times have we seen really nice people grow into fiends? You'd think we'd learn. So do the analysis and turn the tables a bit. Take the needs you have and turn them into what you can give. For example, if you want them to cook for you, take some culinary classes and turn the table. (Like that? Table? Eh?) If you think they're going to meet your needs sexually, read up on intimacy and learn its real language, because what you need right now is not physical. Whatever the need is, find a way to give it

away instead (except for the sex part), and make the giving a strength of yours.

What you'll find is that your need for that thing will be fulfilled as you give it away. The food that comes from your creativity will meet your need for provision. The intimacy you share will meet your need for what you thought was sexuality. The love that moves through you fulfills you. Tons of people have sex before marriage as a way to meet what they think is a need for love. It's not. Intimacy is the need. Get that one right and you'll rule the world. At least your own.

3. You're married
I think you get the point by now. I would just add that this is a long-term development. The choices I made in the beginning were a great foundation, but this unmet need thing is like a time-release capsule. As I get older (49 now), I keep finding deeper needs and ways to give them away. Patience, for instance, or provision. I need these more than ever, but so do my kids and community. I feel stretched beyond my capacity these days. Maybe it's tiredness, or maybe I haven't tapped into deeper wells. In any case, I know that the principle is still true. I need to *be* patient and *be* providing, even when I feel I have nothing. The magic of the thing is that as I do this (via choices, priorities, prayer), it returns to me. So I guess the point here is to persevere, be consistent, and finish well. My needs will never dissipate; they get met and deeper ones surface, which I meet by giving to others, and so it goes on.

Practice:
- *List five or six of your biggest needs. Try to keep the list personal and honest (not "I need money, or a wife", but rather "I've never really understood provision, or intimacy").*

- *What are some ways, right now, that you could give these same things to other people, and what creativity, effort or sacrifice would this require?*

- *What homework would you need to do to develop this in a way that's natural and uncontrived (for instance, cooking classes or understanding children better)?*

- *What do you need from God to help you?*

Nine. Family

Sheryl: You know, like it or not, we're still your family, for better or worse...
*Dwayne: No, you're **not** my family! I don't wanna **be** your family! I hate you fucking people! Divorce? Bankrupt? Suicide? You're fucking losers, you're losers.*
Michael Arndt, *Little Miss Sunshine*

Families are the most complex set of relationships in the universe (I think). In general, I've noticed that people are either moving closer to their family or swiftly running from them. Your family has been the relational training ground of your life. What you experienced through them and observed about them has forged how you will one day respond when it's your turn. For some people, this has been really positive and they're looking forward to having a go. For others, it's complicated. How's it been for you?

When I started out, I was kinda anti-marriage. I thought at the time that I was pretty open to relationships, but in my heart, I was running, hiding behind distractions and activity that kept me busy and kept me from dealing with the issues. I felt that because I was not my father, I'd be fine, and I felt fine. What was missing was context. I am my father's son, and he modeled more than I really wanted to take on, but as kids, you don't get to choose. This stuff has a profound and lasting impact, and what you think will not affect you is really just waiting for context (your turn) in order to come back into the forefront of your life. Before I met Heather, I thought I was okay or neutral, but as I got closer I could see that there was a lot of baggage just waiting to be processed.

For instance, my dad stopped playing with us when we were about seven. Fine. I grow up, as you do, and don't think a thing about it. Get into a relationship, I'm okay, I'm good. I get married, then have kids, and BAM, I don't know how to play with them. I'm blank. Just like my dad. The relational model goes deep, and like it or not, I had to acknowledge that my family background had a huge effect on me (in this issue and many others). So the sooner I got my head around it, the sooner I could start working on family stuff so that the good stuff grew and the baggage got dealt with. My *relationships became the context I needed* to see my deeper issues. So like I said, we're either moving towards family or running away.

The problem: Most of us carry these seeds around with us. Familial experiences bury themselves in our hearts and are just waiting to pop up when the conditions are right. They're not all bad seeds; there may be a lot of positive stuff we probably learned about caring or sacrifice or hospitality, which will emerge when our chance comes. But we  need to be aware that we do not enter relationships neutral on these issues. Part of our "uninformed optimism" is that we think we're gonna be different, based on the idea that we don't want to be like our parents. Not wanting to isn't enough. Here are some things to look out for in yourself:

- *reluctance to get committed (you may think it's about your freedom or "flexibility", but your heart knows it's about pain or not wanting to repeat the dysfunction of your parents)*
- *superficial communication (maybe you never saw your parents argue properly, so you struggle to go deep)*
- *isolation (you like being alone with a person and wouldn't dare introduce them to your family)*
- *fantasy or an idealistic approach towards people (you're trying your hardest to make this thing perfect; you don't want a repeat)*
- *savior complex (you're looking for someone to fix the stuff that's gone wrong, or you're trying to fix someone else)*

Most of the time we don't even know we're doing this. Other people can often see our commitment issues or communication problems, and we're like, "What problem?" We usually don't see it until we have the bigger context. And I mean the whole deal, like marriage and kids and mortgage and all the pressures your parents had when their bubble burst. When you enter into that space, the real you comes out. I encourage you to start working on it now.

Another family issue is learning to deal with how spread out we've become. For instance, living in multiple homes makes it hard to develop a sense of belonging or community. Often our parents, siblings, and extended family all live in different cities (or countries). Even though things are okay between people, there's often no real ongoing connectedness, which tends to leave you homeless and very, very single. So when you try to connect with someone else, it's fine as long as it's the two of you, but when it comes to forming a family, you may not have a healthy concept to build on.

The ways of God: *God is mother, father, sibling, friend, and the God of Abraham, Isaac and Jacob (or the God of generations).* Family is the center of the universe, and while it's fun being single (for a little while anyway), family is the way we really grow up and become our true selves. God has designed this to be an amazing experience if we walk out the principles correctly. The model is unity (us) and diversity (me), freedom (identity) and responsibility (with creativity), which is balanced by seeking the welfare of the tribe above your own. It seems the whole goal of God through the scriptures is to get us all back together as a family, having a great meal in our own garden. But you know, as I write this, it feels flat. Am I not being clever or anecdotal enough? I don't know, maybe it's just pure, childlike stuff we simply need to do to see the wonder of it.

The application: Stop running. Get your head around the fact that having a big huge family one day is a great thing. Not that you need to be married with kids to be happy or complete, but that extended family, whatever form it may take, and your place smack in the center of it is a wonderful place to be. If you can appreciate that, you can start working on the details that'll get you there. For instance, one day marrying into another tribe. Not just those beautiful brown eyes you like so much, but their Mendelian roots (her mom and dad, her siblings, and that weird aunt...). Families also come with expectations and guards you'll have to get through. If you're a family player, they'll most likely welcome you. But if you're looking to take her away and play your own game, you're already on the losing side. Don't make someone choose between you and their family. Be a friend to the whole group, right from the beginning.

When I started spending lots of time with Heather, she wrote to her parents to let them know a little about me. Initially, they discouraged her (South Pacific romance on one hand, strange Californian with a broken family background on the other...), so I dove into the fray. I recorded two 70-minute tapes and sent them from Fiji (where I was at the time) to England (where they were). I explained my family background, my change over the last few years, and my intentions to be an amazing friend. Instead of taking offense, I took their side. They didn't know me from a bar of soap, and here I was spending time with their daughter on the other side of the world, on a ship! They were right to be concerned about my background; they're the gate-keepers of their daughter until they choose to give her to someone worthy enough.

Once we got married, a lot of my own family issues came up: having kids, playing with them, dealing with money, communi-cation and conflicts, roles in the home, sexuality, work/family tensions. Each new step in our marriage brought new contexts in which to manifest (there's an ugly word) my issues. I'm kind of kidding. A lot of really great things were drawn out of me in these situations, but a lot of baggage too. What I tried to do was be aware of them and use the ways of God to process them. Like with the kids and my inability to play with them. The principle is confession: let people know what's really going on. So I did. I sat my little five-year-old Josiah and four-year-old Jordan down to let them know I had no real idea of how to play with them. I loved them to the best of my ability, but I was drawing a blank creatively and emotionally when it came to being playful. The beauty of confession is that most people really appreciate the honesty, even four-year-olds. They told me it wasn't a problem and that they would help their poor father. And they did. The really amazing thing, though, was how the gorilla in the room disappeared. You know, that tense presence that lingers when there's something wrong but people can't talk about it. It's the tension that travels from one generation to the next, strengthened by the silence and inability to cope with the issues. When you share your baggage and work it, you defuse the bomb that's waiting to go off. Through open communication, and the humility to seek change, you can cut off generations of weirdness.

For me this has meant specifically seeking to know God as a parent in order to bring some healing and perspective into my own journey. As I learn from God's model, I apply what I see, and practice things like forgiveness, covering and care, provision. Each time I apply what I'm learning, it slowly becomes me. Over the years, I've become a pretty good father with a decent understanding of family by simply practicing what I see God doing with me. Here are some more examples in the three stages:

1. You're just starting a friendship...
Another aspect of family is that it's so much better to relate to committed groups than just to individuals. Really, the one-on-one stuff in the beginning is romantic, but as time goes on, that one person cannot support your whole life. This is true emotionally, financially, and in a ton of other ways. Having the backup and the care of a family or group of friends will sustain you when it gets tough. The other side of that is true too, like the celebration and hospitality aspects of families that you can be part of. We live right next door to two brothers, one sister (and all the in-laws), eight cousins, and a set of parents, all within a stone's throw of each other. To some, this would be a nightmare, but it's one of the best things in our lives. The way we share meals, rides, and celebrations is as important as the covering and care we provide for each other in the down times. So even if you're single and relating to some friends, get hooked into their families. You have no idea what kinds of good things could be started (including businesses), or what you could learn from this broader, more experienced network of people who have been where you're heading. A three-stranded cord is not easily broken; try that times ten.

2. You're getting really close to making a commitment...
If you are seriously thinking of getting married, try some family counseling. There's a lot of average marriage counseling going on, so try to find people who are super honest, real, and helpful. Read up on family issues and get some bigger perspectives, and don't let the idea of family scare you off. The divorce rate has a cumulative effect; as that rate creeps up over the decades, it obviously has a growing effect on our family lives and values. You may not even know how deeply it affects you or your partner until you really look seriously into it, which, by the way,

hardly anyone does until stuff hits the fan. We naively jump into marriage thinking we won't repeat the sins of the fathers because, well, we don't want to. In reality, we will be what's been modeled to us unless we are proactively working in the other direction. Family counseling (or at least reading up on it) will provide some helpful perspectives that will prepare you for what's coming. If you are serious about being together for the next 60 years, then get a road map.

3. You're married
You probably have been experiencing a lot of the things I've been talking about. So at this point my suggestion would be to track the issues you've really been struggling with and ask: "What are the aspects of God's nature or character that would model a solution for the tough things I'm facing?" For me, this has meant two things. I need to understand intimacy, and I need extraordinary wisdom. I ask for this regularly and practice what I discover as much as possible. It's kept me in the game when I've wanted to give up. It's given me wisdom when I've been clueless.

From the start, I needed a bigger vision of what God originally meant a family to be. I needed something to shoot for, and not just survival. I saw that family was not only the root structure of a community and nation, it modeled the hopes of God in terms of unity and diversity. It was okay for me to be my unique, strange self in the midst of another family. I could learn from and contribute to this new group without becoming assimilated by it. Unity and diversity is an odd but powerful principle, and family is the best place to walk this out. Right now, I'm living in New Zealand in a situation very foreign to my Californian roots. But one of the cool aspects of this new situation is that I'm being extended in myself, and I get to extend them at the same time. Which, by the way, helps me contribute back to my original family at home. My children then synthesize all this into their own international culture. So the overall benefit of diving into family and getting the really big picture has made the harder parts of this journey (getting and staying married) totally worth it.

The last thing I want to mention here has been a huge lesson, modeled to me by Heather's father from the book of Proverbs:

"A wise man builds an inheritance for his children's children."[20]
Thinking of the future, 70 years or so down the track, is almost
impossible in our "internet-time" culture. Thinking and planning
just a couple of years down the road is like pulling teeth for most
people. But the reality is that you'll probably be around for 15
years of your grandchildren's lives. So you're either preparing
for that now, or you're not. What I've learned from Heather's
extended family (and mostly her father, Ray) is that their
planning and consideration, their priorities and choices, and
mostly their heart for their children and grandchildren have all
resulted in a foundation my kids and their kids will build on.
Whether that's financial, spiritual or relational, they have an
inheritance that has been well considered. This was huge for me
to observe, and a blessing to be part of the process. Even better, I
am learning how to do this for my grandchildren (if I have them,
Josiah!). If I want to take the wisdom of God seriously, I need to
plan a long time ahead, and this will be good for all of us.

Practice:

- *List all the really good things you've learned from your family.
  It's good to be reminded of the positive stuff and to build on
  this with your own family.*

- *If you act just like your mom or dad did when you're married,
  would that be a good thing? Not that you will be exactly like
  them, but it's worth considering.*

- *What are some of the family communication strengths that
  you'll be bringing into your relationships? The weaknesses?*

- *What kind of family would you love to have one day? What
  would you need to be working on in yourself to get there?*

- *What do you appreciate or need from God to understand
  familyness better in your life? (I know, familyness is not a word
  —yet.)*

---

[20] Proverbs 13:22

Ten. Sex

I don't know if it's wrong or right
But I don't want to go home alone tonight - I want you.
DJ Jose, "Physical Attraction"
Check it out on YouTube, it's pretty smarmy

Men and women are very different. No, I mean really different. I did the math on this once and figured that at the maximum, a woman can have around 70 children. The world's record is somewhere between 55 and 69 depending on your sources. On the other hand, we have no clear records of how many children one man can father (or should I say "sire"?). Solomon had 1,000 women, so in a good year he could have a few hundred kids. Over his lifetime he could have a few thousand. At the max, a man is capable of having around 18,000 children (my estimate, nobody's confirmed this yet though). So that's around 70 for a woman and around a bazillion for a guy. Like I said, really, really different.

One major difference is our respective biological clocks. On a woman, this is ticking at around 30 days per cycle. For a guy it's somewhere between 30 minutes and 3 days. Why in the world is this so different? Dang! I don't know, but this little bionuisance creates all kinds of "opportunities" to live in an understanding way with each other. Especially if sex is a big deal to you. Not that it should be, but we live in an environment (in the West at least) where the sexualization of our needs has exacerbated all kinds of tensions. Hey, did you ever notice how much "exacerbated" sounds like "masturbated"? My son Levi points this out all the time, as in, "he said 'exacerbated'", and then he giggles.

I think much of the sexual tension that exists in relationships (before and after marriage) is based on a confusion between intimacy and sex. What we really need is intimacy. Emotional, physical, spiritual intimacy. Sex is a subset of intimacy, not the main thing. Most girls get this, most guys don't (initially, but we can catch up). So while the world around us is selling the sexualization of needs, we need a counterbalance. We do have tension, but it's not primarily sexual. Our frustration is largely based on an unfulfilled lifestyle. Our lives are crying out for intimacy, creativity, and true friendship, while popular culture shouts back that it's all about the sex, a primal drive to procreate, or a fantastical opportunity to live with Her Hotness for the rest of our lives. Am I the only one grossed out by how Hugh Hefner looks? You want that?

The sexualization of needs
TV, film, and music are always pumping out examples about how great sex is and how much we need it. I'm not anti-media by any means, but if our real world (home, school, work) doesn't have good models of people in deep friendships and who understand intimacy, then we'll go looking for other worlds where there are all kinds of people waiting to be surrogates for our dreams. A lot of the fantasy examples (like in films) show people who meet, kind of like each other, and then end up sleeping together within a day. What looks like an "instant connection" is pretty much just a physical connection, and one that doesn't last more than a couple of hours, which is the extent of our exposure to their screen-based lives. If sex is the goal, the relational attention span is only good for a couple of hours at best. Now, I haven't heard anyone walking out of the theater saying, "man, I wanna live just like that", but at the same time, this stuff gets into our psyche. Even though we know that a deep, long-lasting connection with someone's soul is the ultimate goal, we still think sex is a massive need or the *quickest* way to make that connection.

The marketplace is another influencer, often filled with false promises of how certain products and services will satisfy you or make you sexier. Overall, most of us are intelligent enough to know this is just hype, and yet I find myself paging through those health mags or looking up at the big screen thinking, "hmmm, I wonder...". I think we all get this, but I just wanna say it out loud, because we put way too much stock in what we think is a sexual need and it comes back on us all the time. So let's agree to call our real need intimacy, and base our conversations and actions on that.

The problem: As we've established, we often replace our need for unconditional love with the need for being physical. Generally, guys learn really early on to replace intimacy with porn, while girls give themselves to boys prematurely to lock in their attention. From these messed-up starting points, we grow up and very little changes. It just goes deeper and the communication gets all layered with innuendo. No one comes out and says what they expect from you sexually, but it's in the back of their minds. These expectations can be cloaked in all kinds of noble or sacrificial language, but at the end of the day, they're still expectations. For instance, a guy will act super sweet, appear to be a great listener, and be all about you, but when you put the breaks on physically, he gets really upset. This may come out as subtle impatience or, in the extreme, date rape. Over time, if these expectations aren't met, people will even drop the relationship thinking it wasn't right for them.

Lame.

For some people, the problem is more addictive. Sexual patterns formed over years can be hard to break, especially if abuse or just hard-core use has been the norm. In this case, humility and honesty with someone can really help, but this has to come from outside of the relationship. You can't bring the really hard stuff into a relationship you're trying to develop. You'll confuse him/her as your salvation and that'll turn into even more complex expectations. The best way is to seek outside help from people who understand addictions or abuse, and let them work the issues with you. You can share this process with those you love (or want to love), but they can't fix you.

I think the main problem with sexuality in developing relationships is our basic impatience. Sex is a wonderful thing, but we don't need it like we think we do. What we need is a deep friendship and camaraderie with someone who gets us and someone we can give to. That takes time, years in fact, so when we emphasize the physical stuff, we undermine the very process that would bring real fulfillment in the long run. And without this healthy process, we think we need sex even more! See the cycle? For me, to have this kind of patience and some healthy perspectives about sexuality, I've needed a wisdom that wasn't tainted.

The ways of God: *God is human/spirit, creative, beautiful, kind, caring, patient.* I believe our sexuality is both derived from and enhanced by these attributes. So the more I understand them and can embrace them, the more holistic my sexuality will be. For instance, beauty on one level (the physical) is simple, but seeing the depths of beauty in character, personality, and soul will make beauty a multidimensional thing that becomes even more attractive. Mix this with a Godly kindness, caring, and patience, and you have the makings of a wonderful sexuality.

The application: No one is starting with a blank slate. In order to be intimate you have to be open and vulnerable, and that starts with honesty. The first step is personal honesty, where you look at the sex versus intimacy problem and deal with the world view and practices you've developed so far. If this is a minor thing, like kissing too much when you were a teenager, then you can make some commitments and start practicing a more patient approach. If you've gone a lot further and haven't been able to really change your behavior, then you may want to get some help from your parents, a counselor or really good friend to whom you can be accountable. This stuff doesn't change overnight. You really want to *establish a new way of dealing with sexuality,* and that can take at least a year or two. And don't try to walk this process out within a relationship. It's not their place in your life right now. Don't be naïve about this. You'll probably just make things worse. I'm not saying you can't be dealing with this stuff and getting closer to someone at the same time. I'm just saying if you try to have that relationship fix the issue, it won't work. Remember, intimacy is found across the wider spectrum of family and friends. If you call on those people to help you be accountable or deal with tougher issues, you won't be lumping the whole deal on one person.

Personal honesty for me meant working through my history and seeing it from a different perspective. At 14 I found some porn mags in the house. This was my introduction to sexuality. Next came the really strange teaching at school (what were those slide shows on about anyway?) and my dad not breathing a word to me on the subject. Not a great beginning. At 18 I had sex with a girl I barely knew at some dive of a party. At 20 I became a Christian and started to work on the lousy foundations I'd built. This meant owning how stupid I'd been and what I thought about it, but I also needed to replace all that with a better understanding. I was blessed by having some really good friends around who were just that. They didn't pressure each other to be "in a relationship", and there was no sexual stuff going on to complicate matters. Just great conversations and doing things that were really beneficial for each other and the city, like running a coffee bar for the homeless in downtown San Jose. This helped me establish a new lifestyle and a better way to relate. It took a couple of years, but I started to see people through the eyes of God and wanted to treat them that way.

At 22 I met Heather and started a friendship with her. Initially, I didn't talk about my past. I didn't need to because I was processing the crappy part with some life coaches and mentors. But after a while, when we were getting close to committing to each other, I let her know everything. This is the next step after personal honesty: sharing with those you're committing to so they know what they're working with. You do this not to be judged, but to start the process of real openness, something you want as part of your relational future. Most people won't reject you for your openness. Quite the opposite usually happens. But they do want to be able to trust you, to know you can own what you've done, and to be prepared for their part in your process. But even more importantly, you've been vulnerable with them and that's what they're looking for.

On top of this you can build the kindness and patience you'll need. For instance, when someone shares their past with you, you'll need to be kind enough to accept them, patient enough to walk out any residual baggage, and creative enough to develop a love that covers them. For Heather and me, this has been a 25-year process. We're doing really well so far, but it's taken forever to get here. I guess sexuality is a healthy result of so many complex connections, getting all of it working together takes a while. Some people can have really exciting sex almost immediately, but intimacy can take decades to develop, and why shouldn't it?

Delayed marshmallows
Waiting for something you really want is an exercise in self-control, with benefits. Walter Mischel has been tracking the idea of delayed gratification since the late '60s. As a professor of psychology at Stanford, he'd bring four-year-olds into a "game room" and place a marshmallow in front of their happy little

faces. The challenge was simple: wait 15 minutes without eating the delicious air-puffed sugarball, and you get another one. But if you can't wait, the first one is all you get. Two-thirds of the children ate the marshmallow within minutes, while one-third distracted themselves, sang songs, and became university professors...

Mischel tracked these children over many years and found that those who had eaten the marshmallow early also struggled with school work later on, had higher BMI's (Body Mass Index, higher usually equals fatter), and found it difficult to maintain friendships. Those that waited scored an average of 210 points higher on their SATs (standard US university entrance exams), were more confident, and generally did better in life. Oh yeah, and they got to eat **TWO MARSHMALLOWS!** The core skill that Mischel identified here was self-control. He found that the kids who could control their urge by distracting themselves managed to put the "hot stimulus" into the back of their minds. They still really wanted it, but they chose to want other things which took off the immediate pressure.[21]

This is a learned skill. Self-control needs to be fostered by looking at the bigger picture and placing higher value on things like trust and a lasting friendship. Sexuality is better when you wait, because in the waiting you actually have time to love all of the other person, not just their body.

---

[21] A useful summary of the findings was published in *The New Yorker Magazine*: "At the time, psychologists assumed that children's ability to wait depended on how badly they wanted the marshmallow. But it soon became obvious that every child craved the extra treat. What, then, determined self-control? Mischel's conclusion, based on hundreds of hours of observation, was that the crucial skill was the 'strategic allocation of attention.' Instead of getting obsessed with the marshmallow—the 'hot stimulus'—the patient children distracted themselves by covering their eyes, pretending to play hide-and-seek underneath the desk, or singing songs from 'Sesame Street.' Their desire wasn't defeated—it was merely forgotten. 'If you're thinking about the marshmallow and how delicious it is, then you're going to eat it,' Mischel says. 'The key is to avoid thinking about it in the first place.'" Jonah Lehrer, "DON'T! The secret of self-control", *The New Yorker Magazine*, May 18, 2009.

1. You're just starting a friendship...
How you deal with sexuality at this stage will set the pace for the rest of your life. If you can't be patient now, not much will change once you're married. If you're feeling an internal pressure, work the issues instead of just looking for some fulfillment. Develop self-control and a caring discipline, and you'll have a good foundation to get you through all kinds of stuff in the future. Spend your time doing better things together. It's not that the sexual side isn't amazing and beautiful; it truly is. But without the foundation of a real love and long-term commitment, it cheapens the whole thing. Without a solid commitment, sex can be destructive, and a lot of you know what I mean. Commitment is about loving them, not using them. Showing patience communicates that all the other dimensions of their personality and character are a bigger priority to you right now.

When you're younger, shallow is fine, like a good party. It's enough to have had a good time. But don't confuse that with the real place of sexuality. The deep connection you build through trust and the long-term faithfulness you establish by being dedicated to someone for decades develop something so rich, it can't be compared to sex without these elements. It may feel amazing to you now, but I promise you, over time you'll regret that you gave yourself to a version of sex that degrades you and the other person. You may think it's okay because you really love each other right now, but I'm saying if you had any real sense of what love was, sex would be the last thing you'd want to do to each other. You also need to remember that your being okay with sex at this stage might be more about your needs (like a lack of love in your family) than about the liberated self you think you are, so be careful. If you want to be led by how cool it feels, then you also have to accept that you're okay with being shallow or driven by your hormones. If you never grow out of this, you'll also be vulnerable to going with whoever offers the best sex in the future, which means your commitments are pretty worthless. On the other hand, if you can respect the power of the sex drive and keep it subjected to a stronger love for other people, then when the time is right, you'll find sexuality to be even more beautiful.

*Note to girls: For the most party, you pretty much lead the physical side of the relationship. You set the pace and give the authority. Be careful with that influence. If you're playing that card to meet your own need or to keep the guy around, you're not focusing on building the lasting elements of a relationship (like patience and faithfulness) and it will backfire on you. If you're responding to what you think **he** wants, then you need to remember that he's relationally retarded and needs to learn how things really work. Use your relational strengths to set the pace and keep the important things in play. If he doesn't stick around because you won't get physical, I don't care how well he plays the guitar, he's not worth your time.*

2. You're getting really close to making a commitment...
This is a hard place to be in. You really like her, you're pretty much married (in your mind, but not her dad's), and you've been so close for so long, you're one kiss away from making babies. Be careful cowboy, because this is where respect (for her and her whole family) and self-control really have to kick in. And some wisdom as well. Having sex with someone you love is the most natural thing in the world. So when you've gotten this far in the relationship, putting yourself in a situation where you're alone and can have sex is simply insane. What do you think would happen? Maybe not the first or second time, but eventually you will do the most natural thing in the world and feel terrible afterwards. And again, not because sex isn't great, but because you know your "yes" needs to be "yes". If you want all of her/ him, then marry them. Until then, you're leaving your options open and it would be cruel to take all they have and not follow through.

I know that some films and ads and books and scientists (by the way, why in the world are scientists allowed to say anything about sex?) say that it's "really not a big deal, sex is natural and should be uninhibited". Free sex has been droned into us for decades and, as advertisers know, repeated communication slowly erodes the defenses. Don't be confused though: if you want the real beauty of intimacy, develop this into a rock-solid commitment. Many prefer diamonds.

Even though I was completely committed to Heather and knew I was going to marry her, I didn't even hold her hand until I'd met her family and had her father's permission to marry her. Once we were engaged, I did kiss her, and probably too much. I should have been much more self-controlled, not because of some Victorian standards, but because I wanted her to know that she could trust me not only now but for the rest of our lives, including when I wasn't going to be around her. Commitment isn't just the engagement; it's being committed to respecting her, her family, and myself.

3. You're married

What we've learned about sexuality over the years is quite simple. Having these massively different biological clocks has meant we needed to focus on how the other person ticked instead of putting pressure on each other to meet *our own* needs. We've had to be patient as we've walked through our own issues, and not demanding of something we couldn't give at the time. We had to realize that we live in seasons, with different priorities, including seasons where sex was not appropriate (like the seven months Heather and I weren't talking to each other). Sexuality is a multifaceted thing, and working all the facets together is much better than the simple act of sex itself.

We've appreciated the beauty of God's creation—in this instance, the humanity of God. But it is all the more amazing when we see all the angles together. The caring goes with the physical, and the patience goes with the physical, and the openness... I could talk a lot more about this but wouldn't want to embarrass my single readers. I know, as if... But the reason I'm being kinda sparse here is that the really important things like patience and understanding are where our priorities need to be. If you have this, the experimentation and revelation that sex can be will be a wonderful part of your future and doesn't need to be prescribed.

Practice:

• *Do you have an issue, addiction or obsession in this area? Are you actively working on the issue and asking for help?*

• *Are any past sexual experiences or issues affecting your present relationship or the way you view the opposite sex? Are you talking with anyone about this?*

• *Are you sensitive to your conscience? Repeated action dulls the conscience, so do you still know when you've crossed a line?*

• *Yeah, I guess the point is to not practice too much, so jump to the next chapter and be good. Remember, 1+1=3*

Eleven. Money

For better, for worse, for richer, for poorer...

Everybody needs money! That's why they call it money!
David Mamet, *Heist*

When you're young, money isn't that big of a deal, 'cause you're spending someone else's. When you get a job, it's still fun and games because now you have even more to play with. But at some stage you grow up, like with house payments or medical bills. All this is kind of daunting for the teenager cum adult, but then you add another person to the mix, their priorities and their way of dealing with money, and things can get really tense. Money turns into a very big deal and can either develop into a solid basis for growth or a constant argument. In their book *Divorce*, Professors Alison Clarke-Stewart and Cornelia Brentano say that for first-time marriages, money is the most frequent source of conflict.[22]

The issue is centered around two people becoming one entity. A legal and financial bond with responsibilities and opportunities. Two people with shared resources and needs. Usually two people who're opposites. Basically, the opposites thing is a good deal. You can be twice as creative and productive and multiply what you have to share with even more people (starting with your kids). But the dark side of being opposites has to be worked out first. You need to know what your financial strengths and weaknesses are, and so does your partner. One weakness (like poor spending habits) can be balanced by the opposite strength (patience and research before buying something). If this is appreciated, you flow together. If not, you annoy each other. After a while the annoying chemicals outweigh the attraction chemicals and you think you're not in love any more. Actually, this is the best time to start loving despite the chems.

---

[22] *Divorce: Causes and Consequences (Current Perspectives in Psychology)*, page 219. The authors also note that in second marriages, children are the most common source of conflict. While the book deals with the causes of divorce, much of it focuses on its consequences, especially for children, which you may want to read through if this has been your experience.

The problem: When you commit to someone, like in dating, it's a variable commitment. You can leave or change your mind. The longer you know someone, the more the commitment grows to cover other things like borrowing cars or money. You entrust things to each other. Sometimes naively, because you're not sure what the transaction entails just yet. So when you loan them money and they forget about it, you're not sure if you should mention it again. Is a "dating commitment" supposed to cover that stuff too? So as your relationship grows, your commitment to each other grows as well, but it's largely through trial and error. By the time you get married, you've committed to sharing each other's resources but you don't really know what that means, which is a wide open door for all kinds of frustration.

Now you have to set priorities. You're committed to each other but you've never shared stuff like this before. So the real values come out and, with them, the surprises. I don't think these problems are deal breakers, but you need to work them aggressively, because money will create huge tensions over time.

Another problem is one person pretending to defer to the other but really becoming financially subservient. If someone doesn't have a clue about money, is afraid of it, or just plain co-dependent, it's easy to let the other person dominate the finances. This may seem like equilibrium for a time, but at some stage everyone wakes up. This may be a woman in mid-life who suddenly realizes that she's got no idea how money works or that she's actually very smart and becomes sick and tired of how *he's* been managing the store. Or he suddenly realizes after 20 years that he's sick of paying all the bills, reconciling the accounts, keeping track of the cash-flow and taking on all the burden and responsibility of the family's finances. Some people wake up very angry.

Heather and I are very similar when it comes to money. We're not big savers and generally don't put a big emphasis on creating financial wealth. We tend to see money as flowing towards the important things, like feeding people and covering the bills. We're responsible, but we're not really proactive. Knowing this about each other was healthy in the beginning. But even with the basics lined up, we found that with each new level of commitment (kids, house, more kids, health) we also had to deal with our different approaches to money. Overall, this isn't a huge problem, but we need some tools to manage our differences and our resources.

The ways of God: *God is creative, material, consistent, providing, resourceful, generous, faithful.* The first thing we had to learn was not to nickel and dime each other over the money we had, but instead to create more. God does not have a poverty mentality but has created an environment where everything multiplies. If you understand creativity and generosity, you'll probably lack for nothing. Another big lesson for me was the fact that God deals in the material world, and this needs managing and stewarding with consistency. When I first became a Christian, I didn't have much regard for possessions. I thought it was all gonna burn, right (WWI, WWII, Nuclear Holocaust, Y2K)? So I never really paid attention to the over 2,500 bible verses about money and what God thought about it.

The application: So I started out not thinking money was a big deal. This is the arrogance of youth. My only responsibility was to stay alive, and that's not so expensive by yourself. Once I got married, things changed fast, which means I needed to change fast. My biggest lessons came from Heather's father, Ray. He had this amazing ability to synthesize full-time service in India as a medical missionary and long-term financial growth and responsibility for his nation of a family. He lived out the principle that "a wise man builds an inheritance for his children's children". Before he left for India, he put a down-payment on a house and bought a small piece of land outside the city. 20 years later, the rents had paid the mortgage and his small plot was now *in* the city. He sold the plot and gave each of his five children an early inheritance so they could make wise investments too.

I was blown away by this full-time missionary wisely using small amounts of money to make a big difference for generations of people. He applied simple principles of careful living, generosity, saving, and long-term planning to be a blessing and a flow of resources. I was  learning fast. We were in a similar situation (full-time volunteers, minus his smarts), so we decided to save for a down-payment on a house which we've now owned for over 15 years. My mom has also been a constant example to us of long-term hard work, faithfulness, and generosity. Learning from those who've lived the life you're about to live is a smart thing to do.

Another application is the principle of God's unity and diversity. Heather and I put our strengths together, along with our children's, to create value. We both work around 10 hours a week each, and this pretty much pays our bills. Sometimes she has more work than I do, and sometimes it's the other way around. We're unified around the principles of living simply (we grow 10% of what we eat, walk everywhere, don't flush the toilets so much...), but we're also super diverse on how we earn our money. Sometimes we argue over stuff (Heather supports bears in China, whatever!), but since we're both earning, we can fight it out on equal grounds. Come to think of it, I didn't even ask her if we could give to KIVA ('cause it rocks!). I don't even think she knows. How male is that.

I think one of the reasons we've not had too many issues with money is that instead of focusing on our lack, we've invested an enormous amount of energy and food in being generous. We both love creativity and hospitality. We take the little money we do have and multiply culinary goodness. We take our space and share it openly with a consistent flow of guests. Not only does this generate good will in return, it creates a quality of life that is blessed by a lack of stress, and stress will kill you. I mean, the medical bills will kill you. But a stress-free quality of life will actually save you all kinds of money. Simple, generous extended family living is a great way to minimize financial burdens.

1. You're just starting a friendship...
So how does money affect "just friends"? At this stage, I would focus on acknowledging where you may be weak, and start thinking long-term. What have you learned about dealing with money and how could you improve on this? Who do you know that you can learn from? Read *Rich Dad, Poor Dad* and *Wealth and Riches*. Get some good financial thinking in your head and learn the formula of (your identity) + (hard work). Money comes from creating value, and this is what you want to be focused on instead of dating, at least for now.

So far, I haven't even mentioned how you do this together, 'cause it's not the point yet. You need to work on developing your creativity, your place in the market, how you'll multiply the resources God's given you. As you do this, you'll gain a broader context in which to relate to your friends, who may just want to start another Bikes To Rwanda[23] program or something similarly cool. If you're working on your own financial ideas and viability, you can draw other people into the process, meaning you'll kiss less and create more. Honestly, people can waste so much time "in a relationship" when they could be changing the world, which is a great way to relate.

2. You're getting really close to making a commitment...
Talk about money. A lot. Start now because this will be a big point of discussion later. See where you agree, where you disagree, and argue about it. See how you argue and how you handle it when the stakes are kinda low. Learn about their financial values and baggage, and how this differs from yours. Don't back off because of the difference; learn to appreciate how this could stretch you.

If you are about to commit to each other, commit to grow in this area as well. How would counseling or a few books help? Who's in your lives that you can go to and ask for their wisdom and experience? Taking the plunge is not just an emotional/sexual dive, it's money and time management and child care and nutrition... so commit to grow in all of these areas. This will broaden your lives and diversify your time in really cool ways, which means you won't be in each other's pockets all the time. Instead, you'll be walking out issues like how to create a budget together, or how to invest 20% of your income in micro loans or your own neighborhood development. Having this kind of financial extroversion buffers your relationship from the kind of selfish myopia that plagues Western families, especially in the early years when you establish yourself as either a consumer or a contributor.

---

[23] Bikes To Rwanda is a program started by Stumptown Coffee Roasters in Portland OR. Check out this amazingly smart and simple approach to fair trade: http://www.bikestorwanda.com

3. You're married

Most of you reading this book are probably better at money than I am (which is why you could afford this). So I'll just offer one tip: Creating a budget that you can both understand and commit to is a good idea. It can be general, if that's how you flow, or very specific. But in either case, make it something you both commit to walking out in the daily use of your shared moneys. You may even agree to have money you don't share, like separate businesses you run. Fine. Just be in agreement. The point is that the budget becomes the third party. If there's a financial problem, take it out on the budget, let the budget be the argument. Because once you agree to it, you can't fudge around with it, which means she can pull me up on an expense that wasn't planned. Budgets create a kind of objectivity that you can hold to.

Ours is very loose. We know we need a certain amount per month and we know where it's going to (mostly food). If it gets out of hand, we rein ourselves in because we have an agreed lifestyle. Personally, I think Heather needs to be more involved in the weekly ins and outs, but she's not keen about the details so, okay, we go on this way. But if I die first, she's gonna have to make up some lost time in the learning cycle.

Finally, we've learned from a lot of couples who are ahead of us in this, that if the wife is not clearly aware of her identity and potential in the marketplace, she needs to start developing this as soon as possible. A lot of people hit mid-life and wake up to their lost potential and get very pissed off. Some leave, some start a new business. I suggest the latter. Work together to create wealth, use the wonderful diversity you've been given. Way too much pressure exists on one or two people to pull in all the income, pay the mortgage, and somehow do well in retirement. As a family, we've been developing a sort of "family economy" where everyone is contributing to the welfare of the group. It's nothing new, just something we've lost in most Western cultures.

Note about agreement: A lot of the problems with money are about agreement on priorities. Being male does not qualify me to make the final decision if we don't agree. So for us, we defer to the one who has the best take on the issue, and if we still can't agree, we don't make the decision. Simple.

Practice:

- *What are your financial strengths? What are your weaknesses?*

- *Who could you learn from immediately (people, books), and will you commit to that?*

- *What are some of the financial tension points you and your partner are facing right now, and have you had the humility to learn from it or are you digging your heels in? Why?*

- *What can you learn from their strengths? What can they learn from you?*

- *Do you have a budget? If not, make one and stick to it for a while. You can adjust it later, but you want to get into the habit of living within boundaries.*

- *How could you and your friends/partner find cool things to give to (like kiva.org) or nurture neighborhood hospitality (like inviting neighbors over for dinner) so that you develop a lifestyle of generosity?*

Twelve. Abuse

*The only thing that holds a marriage together is the husband
being big enough to step back and see where the wife is wrong.*
Archie Bunker, *All in the Family*

There's an old saying that "the woman keeps the home fires
burning". It's a romantic reference to how well a woman can
cook and keep a homely environment ready for her man. Sweet,
eh? The original saying comes from the Roman practice of
chaining wives to the kitchen so they kept fires burning to the
gods, along with all the other slave tasks they had to perform.
This is not far from the barefoot and pregnant idea women have
fought so hard against in the last century. But the really
concerning thing for me is the vague Christian notion of what a
woman's place is in a relationship and in the home. These
notions are largely based on historical Judeo-Christian values
that are rooted in, among other things, old rabbinical prayers
thanking God for not making them women[24], or in the Christian
church's problem with acknowledging women as leaders until
recently. Perhaps the founding mistake in this area has been a
poor translation of Genesis 2:18, where the first mention of a
woman's identity has her labeled "helper" and "suitable" for
man.[25]

These influences, passed down through culture and language,
become an excuse for men to act on their pride and anger, which
leads to abuse. I've also mentioned how a generation of men
raised by women, and bitter against their absent fathers, are
taking out their pain on those closest to them: their mothers and
partners. These subtle yet pervasive excuses start off as mild
forms of communication or emotional abuse. This can easily lead
to chronic (long-term) abuse that slowly destroys another
person's soul by "keeping them in their place" or just denying

---

[24] "Baruch Atah Adonai, Eloheinu Melech ha-olam, shelo asani ishah." ("Blessed
are You, O Lord our God, Ruler of the Universe, Who did not make me a
woman.")

[25] A better translation of the key words "Ezer" and "K'nedgo" for a woman in Gen
2:18 would be "powerful equal" or "saving equal".

them the freedom and support they need to grow. Not that
women need men to grow, but many (especially "Christian-bred"
types) have either agreed with this world view or been sucked by
their own needs into a relationship that they feel obliged to stick
out. Worse still, some women feel that their subservience is
honoring to God.

All this to say… really nice people can get really weird really
fast. An average guy can turn abusive in the right context.
"Christian values", like roles in the home, can easily become a
pretext for control. All kinds of subtle and not-so-subtle
weirdness develops, because these roots go deep, justifying
abusive behavior. This doesn't affect everyone of course, but I'm
always surprised by how lame us men can be. Women can be
abusive too, and when that becomes a dominant issue, I'll
address it. For now, I'm mainly talking to us guys.

The problem: Two becoming one is a massive transition.
Bringing all your diversity into a beneficial unity is a life-
altering process that requires tons of mutual support. But if abuse
enters this delicate balance, the erosion begins.

In general, guys can mess up this process by having a screwed-
up world view that's been dormant until they get married, and
suddenly they feel like they have to "act like a man". Or, if
they've been abused, this new relationship will be the context in
which to unleash pent-up emotions or physical abuse. For
women (again, I'm generalizing), abuse can enter the
relationship via their passivity or subservient attitude and
acceptance of "their place" in the relationship. Added to this,
past abuses can create a wall around their heart which forms a
cocoon against abuse. In either case, abuse (as world view or
experienced) doesn't disqualify anyone from changing, or even
using a new relationship as a platform for healing. But you gotta
go into this with your eyes wide open. If you have no history of
abuse, you still need to be aware of your own potential to abuse
or be abused. If you do have a history of abuse, you need some
solid help to end the cycle.

The ways of God: *God is a healer, wise, powerful (able to
change us), kind, mother/father/friend, just.* I don't have a
history of abuse, but I am very aware of my potential to

dominate in subtle but painful ways. Especially with those who look to me for love and support. It's freakishly evil, how tempting it is to hurt the ones you love. So I monitor this like a nuclear sub and call on God to help me keep an eye on my motives and actions. This is preventative, but an even better approach is proactive, where you are actively *being* just, kind, non-controlling... When you walk in God's ways, you leave very little room for the darker side of your soul to breathe.

The application: As a man, the best response for dealing with abuse is humility. Acknowledging my potential to abuse and being vulnerable to renewing my mind on the issue will make me open to the teaching or advice I need. For instance, I would suggest all guys read a book called *Why Not Women*[26] to get a better world view on the identity and potential of women. This creates a sensitivity to the issue, which for most people will be all that's needed.

For those who have abusive pasts, I would suggest getting some counseling or working it out with a group of friends (if they know what they're doing). Change is possible if there's ownership of the problem and a will to be healed. Most of the growth in my life has come through problems, through hitting a wall and not knowing what to do. I seek God and ask my family and friends to help. I learn and I apply. Growth is more about teachability than it is about having all the answers. Put stuff in the light, be open with people. It's the beginning of change and it flushes out all the dark angles abuse can hide in, waiting to have its turn again in some new relationship. Suffocate the opportunity with honesty. This is really important if you've been abused. You need to acknowledge your likely response. For some, it's aggressive, for others, passive. You need to know how to manage, heal, forgive, and change the situation, and understand how long the process will take. For most people, this will mean counseling. If you're in a relationship, this process will either strengthen it or send them running. Be open and don't

---

[26] This book develops a solid exegetical view of women. It's written by two Christian authors (David Hamilton and Loren Cunningham) who aim to give a biblical view of God that is not anti-woman. This book is not for everyone, but as a lot of abuse stems from our view of God and women, it's worth looking at.

be afraid of losing people; your true friends will stick it out with you.

I'm not going to go through the three phases (before, mid and married) of relationships on this topic. Abuse is a deep issue and needs more qualified support than pages in a book can offer. I will suggest some practice though, just in case you need some help getting started.

Practice:

- *If you do not have an abused or abusive past, you still need to be aware of the potential within. Counter it by understanding the real value of the opposite sex (read some good books on the subject or attend a workshop you think would stretch you in the right direction).*

- *Consider your weak points or acknowledge where you've been dominant in the past. Apologize.*

- *If you have been abused or abusive, start with some friendly counseling from an elder, or get professional help. Counseling is not just for the extreme cases of mental illness. There are some deep issues here and professional counselors know how to unlock, manage, and prescribe a way out.*

- *Ask God for wisdom and healing **as part of the overall process** (meaning, God doesn't usually work alone; add this strand to the other help you get).*

Thirteen. Everything all at once

If you can keep your head when all about you
Are losing theirs and blaming it on you...
Yours is the Earth and everything that's in it
Rudyard Kipling, "If"

As men, we generally consider ourselves to be strong. We can move boxes and stuff. But when it comes to relationships, I'm always amazed at my lack of stamina. I can usually deal with any one of the last seven issues I've mentioned, but if two or three of them come at me all at once, I collapse like a house of cards. Honestly, it's like the power gets drained and all I wanna do is leave or hide. Maybe I'm unique in this, but when I look at the checkout rate (break-ups or divorce) and see the men-to-women leaving ratio, it seems we men aren't that strong after all.

Facing a bunch of difficulties all at once is hard for men and women. Still, I think women often have an edge when it comes to dealing with multiple issues.[27] In any case, all of us need to consider where our relational stamina has gone. It's like we've lost our ability to deal with pain or tension. We're so attuned to our own needs being met that when this nerve gets pinched, we instantly feel like we're in the wrong place and the only solution is to find greener grass.

I've mentioned before that Heather and I had an argument that led to over seven months of not speaking or even really relating to each other. Typically, these kinds of arguments are simply the last brick on top of a ton of bricks. In the months leading up to this, I'd been reviewing the last 10 years of my life and had become very disappointed with the results. At the same time, I'd been dealing with the chronic pain and depression of never really having a father around to help me through the various issues of

---

[27] In general, women seem wired to multi-task. For instance, the *Corpus callosum* is the shaft of nerves that joins the two halves of the brain. A woman's is generally thicker than a man's, which many believe is the basis for a woman's multi-tasking abilities. Also, pound for pound, women are usually stronger than men (it's just that we're bigger), and they learn to focus on relationships much earlier then we do. So yeah, I think they have an edge that we could learn from.

growing up and getting older. On top of that was the sheer
fatigue of having run 25 courses and traveled to 30 countries
over two decades. Oh, and there's the small matter of raising
four kids (home-schooling them in four countries including
Germany, the only place in the EU where it's illegal). And to
finish it all off, I had an international move. Psychologists say
that after a death in the family or divorce, moving to a new
country is the third-highest stress factor in a relationship.

Like a ton of bricks.

The problem: They say that what doesn't kill you will make you
stronger, right? Who the hell are these people? Probably Navy
SEALs, and I bet they're amazing at relationships too. Or not.
Anyway, I do think problems can help you grow, and yet
knowing this has not always helped me find the grace to deal
with the issues. Here are some things I think make this harder:
- *The Church's emphasis on "my personal Jesus":* Jesus is
  supposed to make you happy, right? So when things get hard,
  that thing must be wrong. So we leave because hard = wrong.
- *A drugged-up generation grows up:* In the '60s, a painful world
  was drowned out by sex, drugs, and rock-n-roll. A lot of these
  guys grew up and now give Ritalin to their sugar-soaked
  children while Prozacking or Valiuming themselves to keep
  things cool. We've developed a culture of medicating pain
  instead of preventing and healing it.
- *The Law:* It's amazingly easy to break a commitment. The
  State makes it a simple matter of paperwork, the church is
  kinda compromised due to internal dysfunction, and divorced
  parents give tacit permission through their actions. You have all
  the authority you need to avoid any relational pain.

There's more, but add these few things up and it's easy to see
why we have so little moral fiber. Ooh! Moral fiber, that's
another reason. The church has talked about moral fiber,
character, fidelity... for years. Preached on it, sold books on it,
raised money on American TV from it, just about everything but
modeled it. At least, it often seems that way. There's certainly a
huge disconnect between the expectations of the "faithful" and
how life is lived; the divorce rates alone within the church attest
to that. Weeping pastors on TV, girls tossing their chastity rings
or Christian guys being all too willing to steal some virginity all

point to the fact that a lot of us don't practice what we preach. Where in the church today is the quiet witness of a pure and loving life? The model is busted.

We have to dig deeper and find an original strength. Part of this strength comes from understanding the place of pain in our lives. Pain is an amazing blessing. It keeps us from destroying ourselves and is part of our biology and psyche for good reasons. Misunderstanding its place turns us into relational lepers, unable to feel pain and therefore destroying ourselves and the bonds we need. Pain and pleasure happen to be in the same nerve endings. They complement an incredible balance that keeps us healthy. When hard issues come up, the pain we feel is meant to sharpen our response. Dodging the issue only prolongs the lesson. So hard isn't wrong, it's just hard. Coping with pain will have an amazing benefit, but having the ability to cope, given the many strikes listed above, requires some supernatural help.

The ways of God: *God is unconditional, accepting, giving, patient, and works in seasons.* The root of God's commitment towards us is the unconditional way we're treated. It's not based on our performance or attributes; it's just pure love without demands. I should note here that many people have lived under religious demands their whole lives, but they've not come from God. These perceptions of earning God's love come from fear-mongering, controlling religious people and institutions that need to maintain the allegiance of their flock to keep paying the bills. God's love is unconditional, accepting, and patient.

Note: I know I've made a few critical remarks about religious control and money. It's an age-old problem. Take away the money from the scenario and things would clean up really fast. Having said that, I think it's essential for people to come together (fellowship) and learn from each other, to support each other and facilitate each other's ongoing development. I'm just bugged about the control and the money, not the getting together.

Tapping into the unique power of this love has been the biggest challenge and reward of my life. Not that I've nailed it, but I know how to walk in it and am learning to make it a normal part of my life. Also, this unconditional approach has been the only thing keeping me in the game when all the issues hit me at once.

It's like the storm is raging, and the only way to survive it is to walk on water.

The application: walking on water: So things start to get rough. Past abuses rise up, unmet needs, demands on your time, sexual problems, money issues, pride... they all start to take their toll. It's like a relational storm and you feel like the only way to cope is to leave. But you can't really leave a storm; you have to go through it, because even if you could duck out of the relationship, nothing's really changed. And when you stop blaming other people long enough, you'll see that you carry the same baggage from one relationship to another. You have to go through the storm to change all that.

God sees the storm and our fear. It's real and it's hard. Then we hear this voice calling us out of our protective stance and into the midst of the hard stuff, with an extroverted heart. To love them, not us. To hear and see their pain and opportunities. And so we try, we stand and move towards the difficulties. It's hard as hell but we shake off the myriad excuses pouring through our minds and simply love instead. We listen more than being heard, we identify, empathize, care... We endure. We absorb pain and press through it to offer something better. And slowly, we notice that we're above the elements, outside of our own pain and need. This place we've created through caring and patience has formed a peace in us. We get stronger, able to carry more, able to endure more, and after a while we understand that the love that has been flowing through us, unconditionally, is loving us too. As it moves through us to meet the needs of others, it's been meeting our needs. It's the love of God, and its power is all-encompassing. By simply choosing to stand and move into the storm, we've activated a catalytic response in our own lives. In giving, we've received.

I mentioned earlier that Mihaly Csikszentmihalyi's principle of flow shows that people who've entered the zone of their own creativity start to lose awareness of themselves. Mihaly (can't even pronounce his last name) has shown that part of this "out-of-body" sense is based on our bandwidth. Apparently, we have a limit to the amount of stuff we can process at once. So a jazz musician who's deep into an improvisational riff may be using so much of her processing bandwidth that she doesn't *realize* her *self* in the process. There's simply no more room for the awareness bits (self conscious, need for food or water...). And apparently, it doesn't matter. People who have found this place of flow say that the flow itself is its own reward. Maybe we're actually wired to be creative in such a way that all our bandwidth is used on the art and not the self. Maybe one of the reasons we're so self-centered is that we're not using our bandwidth on creativity? I dunno, it's just a theory.

Maybe it's bandwidth, or maybe it's the power of creative love, but either way, when you put all your energy into other people, you lose a sense of self (the baggage part) and gain the reward of that love moving through you. By the way, this does not mean becoming a doormat for other people. I'm primarily talking about handling stress when everything comes down on you. Being extroverted, or as Rookmaaker says, being "centrifugal"[28] in your approach to creativity and love, allows you to enter the place of flow. And it's really hard to be abused when you get there.

Practically, it looks like this: All kinda crap can be going on around me (or caused by me), so I breathe deep and I stay put. I don't leave or check out. I determine to listen, or apologize, or communicate better. I don't leave. I listen some more, for the need behind the words. I may confuse things, or jump to conclusions, but I don't leave. I try to understand the timing of things. I stay engaged, or give room, but I don't leave. The more I can see or hear my wife or kids or friends, the less I focus on my stuff. Even if I'm justified, it's not the point, because touting my stuff is not going to help. Then the magic happens. Somehow in the midst of my fast-talking, prideful, smug, needy, irritating self, I start to see *them*. By staying put and listening, I see beyond the attack to the cry. I see the person behind the need and how precious they are, beautiful even in the argument. I see the value of them and I reach out to that value to bless it. The closer I get to it, the more my position gets put into perspective. The

---

[28] Rookmaaker makes the point that certain artists are "centrifugal" in their approach, meaning that as they create for the community, the art goes out from them to the community, and the fame is in the work itself. Centripetal art, on the other hand, is where the fame of creativity goes to the artists. *Art Needs No Justification*, Inter-Varsity Press.

more I listen, the more I hear, and the less I'm distracted by my baggage. I'm not drowning in the water; I'm on top of it.

If I can choose something loving at this point, like an apology or some action that says a thousand words, then I set into motion that catalyst, and now I'm flowing. Like a few years ago, when my son and I were at each other daily, arguing over seemingly nothing but still *always* arguing. I determined to try harder, listen more, and DO SOMETHING that would kick this flow into gear. I took him on a trip with me to Seattle where he ended up getting a job. We hung out together for a couple of weeks, sleeping in the same room together, like camping. The conversations moved from arguments to memories and family. The pressure was lifting and we were hearing each other again. I chose to encourage instead of challenge. I facilitated instead of attacked. On the last day of being there, I had got some stuff (laundry detergent, toothpaste...) for his new place and went down to his room to drop it off. I was going to pray a blessing over his bedroom, but before I could get a word out, I started crying like a baby. All of the tension was coming out and I couldn't stop for two hours. Later that evening I was eating a burrito at Chipotle's on the Ave near the University of Washington. I still had red eyes, but as I watched the young students walk past, I noticed something about their spirit. It was so weird, but I could see something of their relationship with their parents. This one had a bitter chip on his shoulder, that one deeply loved her dad, another was playing with life and hurting himself... I had somehow come into a zone of seeing things I never noticed before. Once I lost my lame priorities, I started to notice so much more.

Unconditional love

> If I speak in the tongues of men and of angels, but have not love, I am only a resounding gong or a clanging cymbal. If I have the gift of prophecy and can fathom all mysteries and all knowledge, and if I have a faith that can move mountains, but have not love, I am nothing. If I give all I possess to the poor and surrender my body to the flames, but have not love, I gain nothing.

Love is patient, love is kind. It does not envy, it does not
boast, it is not proud. It is not rude, it is not self-seeking, it
is not easily angered, it keeps no record of wrongs. Love
does not delight in evil but rejoices with the truth. It
always protects, always trusts, always hopes, always
perseveres. Love never fails.
1 Corinthians 13

This is the only thing in the universe that will hold you together
when everything comes down on you all at once. It's not about
protecting your heart or your interests. That's impossible. But
love like this, unconditional care for others, will activate a
powerful grace in your life. You can still be hurt, and will be, but
now you're working on a whole new plane. You'll learn about
patience by seeing that people are worth waiting for. You'll learn
about acceptance by losing your expectations of others and, in
doing so, appreciating them even more. You'll learn about how
love takes seasons, and that they're all worth the timing and
diversity each one offers. By choosing to walk on water like this,
you'll find that love really does protect, trust, hope, and
persevere. And I guess even more importantly, your love will not
fail.

Practice:
• *Don't leave, don't give up.*

Part 3: Working it out. Practical ways to make this real in your life.

Chapter fourteen is about laying some good foundations...

Chapter fifteen talks about practicing unconditional love with God...

Chapter sixteen talks about practicing with your family...

Chapter seventeen talks about practicing in your neighborhood...

Chapter eighteen talks about practicing with your best friend (guy/girl relationships)...

Chapter nineteen is a letter to my son...

Fourteen. Laying the foundations

The life I touch for good or ill will touch another life, and that in turn another, until who knows where the trembling stops or in what far place my touch will be felt.
Frederick Buechner

I repeat: Unconditional love is something we create. It's come from the Divine, it flows through us, and our needs get met as we give this love to others. So far so good. We've addressed a number of issues and foundations in our lives that will make this doable, so now let's look beyond the baggage and into the possibilities. In turning away from the orientation of people loving us, seeing us, speaking our love language, we can turn towards our relational strengths and start developing them. If we're to create love, what are the basis and ingredients of that creation, and are we prepared for the process?

As I mentioned before, love is not something you find. What you do find are many opportunities to create love where it doesn't exist or needs a little help. And there are more opportunities than you may think. The following chapters will look at some of the relational possibilities with God, in your family, your community, and with your close friends. These are the hard-core, everyday kinds of opportunities that will exercise and grow your ability to love. It's in these places that your criteria (the long lists of things you want others to be for you) changes into meaningful values. Where your selfish orientation gets suffocated in the wonderful exchange of meeting other people's needs. Where you lose the fantasy about finding love and instead create hundreds of small but important ways to give love.

But in order to do all this, a few things need to be in place, especially since we're trying to call down something supernatural into our lives and counter a culture obsessed with its own entitlement. We also need to find a way to wrap all this into and express it through our natural identity. This is not a typical process, but with these aspects in place, the power of God's love can flow unhindered through our lives.

1. Losing the empty theology

Not everyone reading this book will consider God a central part
of their life. So I just want to say here that as I talk about the role
of God in unconditional love, I'm doing so from my own
experience. Without a spiritual connection to something higher
than myself and my issues, I couldn't practice the flow of this
love in the ways I've already mentioned. It's from the
recognition that I am not an island, and that my Creator has a
better love to offer, that I make the next few points. I hope, in
any case, that this perspective will encourage you to consider
God in another light.

We mentioned before that a lot of the principles of God have
become fairy tales. Either because of the lack of good models, or
simply because we've dumbed down the story, we have lost the
power of a centrifugal love. The way God models this is showing
concern and practical love for the poor, the disenfranchised, the
ones not being loved now. The quickest way to put this right in
our lives is loving our neighbor as ourselves, and especially our
neighbor in need. Not just the cute guy who works at the library,
but the person you may feel awkward being around. Our
theology has often agreed with the spirit of entitlement ("name it
and claim it"), and we need to reverse this. And the coolest thing
is, no one needs to teach you anything to get started. Firstly,
because you already know it, and secondly, because loving other
people in practical ways is the simplest concept in the world. No
seminary education required.

A lot of very organic and helpful projects are springing up
around the world based on a simple love for God and neighbor.
A friend of mine, Mark Scandrette, has developed all kinds of
cool workshops that he runs in the Mission district of San
Francisco. He collaborates with his neighbors to figure out how
to deal with money and art and crime. He's well connected with
his surroundings and links all this to an intentional theology of
care and wisdom from above.

Wherever you find your faith has become a head game, find
something practical to do with it and things will sort themselves
out really fast. The ways of God are so simple, kids can
understand them, so none of this is complicated. It's our selfish
interpretations that have made things weird. Like people telling

you to pray for your future spouse... What the heck is that about? Instead, how about finding simple and helpful ways to love your neighbor; at least that's in the bible.

2. Serving others by being yourself

We've spent most of our lives learning to be something for other people. We're trained to respond to social prompts and change our looks, attitudes, and behaviors to comply. All along the way, we lose a sense of who we are and how we naturally love. The only way I've been able to give unconditional love is on one condition: it needs to be from my heart. By this I mean I need to express love in a way that's integral with who I am. My identity, my creativity, my style of communication... all the ways I express myself. This is the gift I give to others.

I talked about how misleading "love languages" can be in Chapter Six, but I just want to mention here again that you cannot love someone else the way they want for your whole life. You can put a ton of effort into a sacrificial approach, but it won't have the same effect as when it's coming from your real skills. The best way to sustain unconditional love is if it comes from your heart and identity. I know it sounds sacrificial to serve regardless, but if you look at those who've been super effective in their service, it's because they are totally wired to love in that particular way. Look at how Bono and Jeffery Sachs have had an impact on poverty. They're not running orphanages, they're using the "currency of celebrity" (Bono) and massive economic brain power (Sachs) to facilitate fathers taking care of their own children. They're loving with their own language.

I take time to work with artists and neighbors in my community. I do some life coaching, some teaching, and some practical service. Right now, we're working on creating a neighborhood portrait for a local cafe using a 1958 Leica and producing 40 old-school (B&W film, traditionally enlarged onto fiber-based prints), hand-painted images that represent the people of our town. I could do this my whole life and get better and better each year, because this love is tapping into my real identity as a coach, father, and creator. And if I can do this for people across the street, I can do this with my future family. You're called to be yourself, and this is the basis for a sustainable love.

3. Consistently creating, consistently giving

Based on the idea above, you take your identity and gifting to create value in the community. Through your work and service (and your work should be service) you're developing good things for people who need them. This could be something as simple as a better cafe or small business or, over time, something larger scale, like educating people about how banking or healthcare is done. As you develop your space in the market, you keep finding new ways to share this with others. Could be by employing other people, teaching, starting a new band... Just giving your time and resources to people who need it. This kind of collaboration is good for everybody.

As you develop a lifestyle of creative generosity, you're moving towards a kind of wholeness and fulfillment. The upside is that you won't be a selfish co-dependant looking to suck the life out of others because you don't have one. I think most people who foolishly move into relationships too quickly, for whatever reason, are bored and lifeless. Or stressed and lacking a creative wholeness. So put your identity to work, make stuff you love, share it with others, and you won't be so vulnerable to the "date and fail" cycle. In fact, you'll be a large tree planted by streams of water, where your branches cover other people, where your life becomes a living example and model which other people would like to be part of. You'll be a pretty attractive prospect too, so you're gonna have to deal with people wanting to marry you pronto. But that's no problem; just tell them to read this book, 'nuff said.

4. Seeing other people, hearing other people

The last foundation I want to mention here is a bit of an art form. Learning to see other people, their depth, the layers of their character, and taking the time to really hear them is so hard to do. Most of us only see what we're looking for. We only listen to when people stop talking so we can say our part. I think we do this because of our insecurity. We keep a kind of forcefield around our lives by always presenting *me* but rarely seeing others for who they are. If we did the latter, it would become about them.

This is why the first three foundations (a better view of God, serving by being yourself, and constantly creating) are so important. It gives us the infrastructure for a solid security. Once we have this, we have the psychological basis for hearing and seeing others. The next step is the hard part: the practice. If you're used to checking people out, or having monologues in your head while other people are talking, then you have to renew the spirit of your mind. And let me just say, it's totally worth doing, because when you really see and hear other people, you open up to their wonder and beauty and amazingness. You also broaden the scope of who you thought you could connect with. And finally, you're treating others how you would like to be treated.

Here's how you renew the spirit of your mind in this area.
1. *Acknowledge your "checking people out" tendencies, or your lack of hearing and seeing others. Apologize to anyone you feel you need to. This builds sensitivity.*
2. *Commit yourself (before God, if that's helpful) to be a person who truly sees and hears other people.*
3. *Catch yourself and acknowledge, on the spot, when you are checking people out or just not listening.*
4. *Focus on them, listen intently, ask better questions, focus some more...*

If you do this repeatedly, over a year or two, you will develop this art. It's not easy but it is doable. I've found that renewal in any area of my life takes about 12 to 18 months. It takes this long to establish a completely new pattern. But at the end of that time, I'm not trying to be different, I *am* different.

I know I'm throwing a lot of things at you. Some of these things need some real consideration or even soul searching. Maybe even counseling, or just a committed process so that you're building good foundations in your life. Don't rush through these ideas looking for some clever approach to dating or whatever. I'm sure you've seen by now that this is not that kind of book. Take the time to digest, apply what you can, and then digest some more. Real learning comes through commitment, education, and then application. Give yourself the time and space to go through this well. Also, don't try to force this into a relationship you're in now, because you may rush through it all trying to "get it right". Learn to be comfortable with your own pace and process, learn to love your family and your neighbors. Be a good brother, sister, friend, and in time you'll become a great husband, wife, father, mother.

Fifteen. Practicing with God

*The spiritual life does not remove us from the world but leads us
deeper into it.*
Henri J. M. Nouwen

Live your beliefs and you can turn the world around.
Henry David Thoreau

I need one consistent person in my life to whom I can relate. A
person who gives me a steady bearing. A person who will
challenge me and accept me at the same time. A person who
never changes and yet is dynamic enough to excite my soul. I
need someone I can talk my head off to and still be comfortable
being silent with. I need to confess my stupidity and weakness,
and also have someone to encourage me to new levels of
creativity. I need an amazing source of love so I can give it away.
God is the only person I can do all this with, and because of this
relationship I have a reference for all the others in my life.

It may sound kinda cheesy, but for me it's not. For me, this is a
radical kind of faith that connects me to a Divine love. Faith that
translates into conversations and actions with God that then flow
into the rest of my life. This is hugely different from simply
holding religious beliefs. Today, it's like belief has become a
kind of badge, a set of ideas that, if we hold to it, gives us a place
in church or in heaven. But faith is very different; it must be
acted on. So if I say I love God but don't love my brother (or
wife or kids), I'm just being religious, touting my beliefs. But
when I act on my love for God and my brother, I'll understand
who God is and so will those around me.

So practicing love with God is an active challenge for me. It
challenges my selfishness and myopic priorities pretty
constantly. And this affects my relationships every day. For
instance, every Sunday night we have an extended family
gathering. There's around 15 to 20 people who show up from
Heather's nation of a family along with my sister and her fam.
Overall, it's an amazing thing that's become a family tradition.
But it's also kinda hard for me to be part of for a number of
reasons, so I often don't show up. Last Sunday night I was

tending the fire and petting our huge white Maremma (Italian sheep dog) and chatting with God about my reserve in going to "Sunday Tea". God said nothing out loud, but was kinda reminding me in my soul about being a son, family, being a part of something bigger than myself...

So I went next door and kissed my father-in-law, sat down in the living room and joined into the conversation. Practicing. After a while Heather's mum brought out some letters Heather had written 40 years before. They were pretty cool, but then her mum told us about the time Heather crossed over the Khyber Pass into Kabul where she stayed with Chris Anderson's parents (the guy that runs TED) and went shopping for some fishnet stockings. In Kabul! In 1969!! How cool is my wife. I would have missed all that if I had not been practicing. In fact, I would have missed Heather altogether if I had not been responding to God's challenge for me to understand unconditional love some 26 years earlier.

Taking risks
Another way I practice is being open and honest with God. I know that sounds really basic, but I'm amazed at how people can know each other for years and still not be open or honest with each other. Practicing these really simple foundations with God makes it more natural when you need to be open with the people in your life. And I'm not talking about confession or a religious conversation about how bad I am all the time. My practice is taking a long walk and conversing about the range of things going on and how I'm affected by them. It may end up in praying for something, asking for advice or just pondering stuff together. It loosens the channels between my heart and mouth, so that when I'm with Heather, or with friends, or teaching, I can be more open because I have this secure place I can go to, vent, and be accepted.

Any relationship is a risk. Being known, sharing money, physical vulnerability... it's risky business getting close to someone. But all the relational risks I've been able to take have been founded on taking risks with God. The acceptance God offers created a platform for me to extend myself way outside my comfort zone. As mentioned earlier, I met Heather on a ship in the South Pacific doing relief work in seven different nations. I was a totally different guy from the one most of my high school friends ever saw. I almost got shot in Guatemala, rescued young girls from sleazy bars in Tahiti, slept next to the smokestack on the roof of a small ferry navigating by stars through the Tongan Island group, all based on taking risks for the love of God. It was an amazing adventure followed by the adventure of getting married and having kids. By the way, the kids part was scarier than the shotgun in Guatemala.

God has taken huge risks in relationship with us. Giving us the earth, he allowed us to screw things up, and still stayed connected to us, committed to us. This is the model I apply in my extended family and community. I don't go into relationships that will be safe, or perfect. I take risks to love people and then see what happens. It was a pretty big risk getting closer to Heather. I wasn't really approved of initially by the family (nobody knew me, and I get this, 'cause I'm super cautious with my kids), and I had a lot of baggage that was discouraging me from wanting to be in a relationship. But after jumping into the God thing boots and all, it wasn't that hard to deal with some of my internal stuff and be intentional with Heather. So risks aren't about going up to that person on the bus and telling them that you've been watching them for the last two years (weirdness!), it's about responding to the challenges God gives you and learning to try, and fail, and still be loved. Get this down and you can share it with the world.

Fellowship
I think most of us need a radical improvement in how we practice loving and being loved by God in groups. A lot of religious fellowship environments are passive. You sit, you stand, you kneel on the prompts, and you listen a lot. I think there's a place for this, but in a world that desperately needs to see the love of God in tangible ways, we should be looking for more creative opportunities to express God's priorities. For instance, Wesley developed accountability groups of five or six people who regularly shared the challenges in their lives and committed themselves to active change. Wilberforce had a fellowship in Clapham that wrestled with the issues of slavery and eventually led to international change. A group of friends around the corner from where I live started a cafe, cooking

classes for local immigrants, and an artists' fellowship, simply to love a square kilometer within Auckland.

I could go on and on about the many organic, relevant ideas I've seen people apply. But I also know many other people who continue in a very selfish social model. When it comes to creating relationships, the selfish types start scanning for love because they've skipped the real stuff with God and neighbor, and head straight for the kill with Naomi or whoever. Our churches are becoming social *scenes* loaded with typical dating agendas. How about doing something really amazing in the community together with people, and getting to know them that way. Coffee and donuts? We can do better.

The final thing I want to mention here is how we live with God at home. Whether you're flatting or living in a family, your home is the place where the important ways of God need to be expressed. Hospitality, creativity, care, teaching, provision... all start in the home. Even if you just have a room in an apartment, it can be a good training ground for learning about God and loving others. We do this in a number of ways as an established family, including having 20 to 30 people stay with us each year from a few nights to a few months. But when I was 21, it was in a house with seven other guys near San Jose State University. We shared a cooking schedule, had guests over all the time, and ran bible studies and a homeless center in town, all to figure out a little more about God. We practiced the presence and priorities of God in the small things, every day, so when I went on from there, it was a little more natural. I've lived in 22 homes since then (a lot in the early years and only three in the last 14), and each one has been a place of hospitality and creative care for people in the community.

Whether it's making a special meal for local social workers or teaching a bunch of fathers about rites of passage for their teenage kids, our home has been where we've learned more about the love of God than any place else. So if you want to get married and have a great family/home environment, start with the place you have now. Be faithful with the little you know about God, through practice, and the rest will come naturally.

Practice:

• *In which ways could you improve your relationship with God today? (Be simple and practical; lofty goals aren't met all at once.)*

• *For each thing God is giving you, teaching you, how could you give something similar to those around you? (And don't go dating someone and calling it a "ministry" to them; that's just weird.)*

• *What better way could you be relating to others in small groups that gives to the community instead of taking them away from it?*

• *How are you relating to God at home and what could you do immediately to improve this?*

• *How can you share your space with others in a meaningful way?*

Sixteen. Practicing with family

Family life is full of major and minor crises—the ups and downs of health, success and failure in career, marriage, and divorce—and all kinds of characters. It is tied to places and events and histories. With all of these felt details, life etches itself into memory and personality. It's difficult to imagine anything more nourishing to the soul.
Thomas Moore

A lot of people jump into a new relationship as a way of trying to move past the pain and complexity of their own families. Like, "maybe this time things will be better". It's amazing to look at the speed in which people leave their families behind and the distance they add as a buffer between them. This may not be you, but perhaps you could ask yourself: "Am I moving towards my parents with my relationships and future plans, or away from them?"

You can only multiply the quality of your own life, and that includes your history. What you don't deal with, you multiply. You may not think that's the case because everything seems fresh (new town, new people, new him or her). But as time goes on, context develops. The same context that added tension and exacerbated the internal issues of your parents. When your context includes money issues, children, and health problems, be prepared to see how much like your parents you really are. Which isn't necessarily a bad thing. There's probably lots about them that you're already appreciating in your own life. I guess I just want to encourage you to not run from the negative stuff. You have to go through that stuff to change it.

I'd like to go over six things I've learned going through my family context. I wish I'd known this stuff starting out. Maybe it would have kept me from wasting all the time I spent running from my roots.

1. Dealing with the past to prepare for the future
As I've looked over the long-term relationship with my family, I've noticed this trend: Parents start out as care givers and end

up as dependants; children start out as dependants and end up as care givers (or pay others to care for their parents).

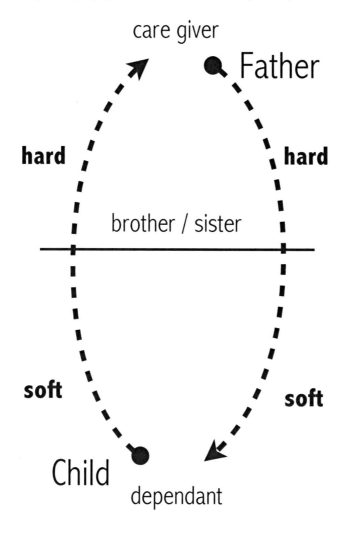

The trick is to stay connected during this cycle, because it's really easy to drop out. Especially when life gets hard for our parents and they take it out on us. I'm not trying to sound all emo here, but children can't help but be affected by their parents' stress over finances, unfaithfulness, or just the hardness of life. So even though we start out soft, we get hardened over time as a means of protection or payback. The bummer is, as time goes on, parents eventually get soft, like a retired father who wants to reach out to his daughter again. But these efforts are often rejected by the hurt or confused daughter or son.

This hardness passes from generation to generation, and even though you start off "open" towards relationships, after a while the hardness comes back and you're making the same mistakes as your parents. I eventually saw this in myself about five years after leaving home. So I determined to arrest the cycle and stay super connected, especially to my dad. I prayed, wrote letters, visited, and made sure I was not letting go. I wanted to be soft when he got there. And he did. It took my dad five years to respond to my letters, 10 years to have normal conversations, and after 15 years we had some full-on reconciliation and forgiveness.

Now imagine if I'd not been aware of this cycle of dependence and care? I would have become harder and harder towards him, which would also affect my other relationships. I would have avoided marriage altogether or, even worse, taken this tension out on my wife and kids as time matured the issues festering in my heart. So I suggest you track where you and your parents are on this scale, and stay connected. This leads to the next lesson.

2. Takes two to tango

Sometimes we get a revelation about family issues and want to dive in and make things right so we can get on with our lives, sans the baggage. We're eager because we're just forming our relational foundations, but they're loaded with all kinds of complexity which will take years to unravel. At first, I wanted my dad to dive into the issues with me, but I was completely unrealistic. He had developed bitterness over his father's divorce, fear about his own health, and tons of work-related stress providing for a large family. Over the years, this stuff adds up, and I was not taking it into account.

My dad needed time to work on these things. He needed to know he was accepted either way. He also needed to see the results of his own actions and how this affected us. Aside from the acceptance, I couldn't provide any of the key elements to change his heart. I needed to work within *his* timeframe, which was frustrating at first, but I soon learned that this didn't have to stop my own growth or change. As long as you're working the issue proactively, you'll keep that hardness from setting in your own heart. I needed to keep my commitment to him alive and stay connected in any way I could. I needed to keep praying for him, communicating when he could take it, and visiting when appropriate. Eventually (15 years later) he invited me and my brother out to dinner, where he apologized for a ton of things, and so did we.

All this created a basis for me to understand the timing and acceptance of two people trying to work things out. Which is exactly what I needed to really love Heather. It gave me a process in which to ventilate my tension with my father, without taking it out on my new relationships, like with my kids. Understanding and applying the timing of change defused the bomb that was waiting to go off in my own family.

3. The allowance to change
I left home when I was 18 and traveled around the world, got married, and changed heaps. But whenever I visited home I noticed a trend: I was often expected to be the same person I was before I left. For my family, this meant me being a lazy teenager who just sat around watching TV and not being helpful at all. Even if I wanted to be different, the expectations were so heavy, I found I could easily slip back into being that useless slob.

Expectations are a powerful thing. It's like the power of a spoken word; when someone encourages or discourages you, it goes deep. If people think of you in a certain way and hold that over you, especially people who know you really well, it's super hard to change or be different around them. The easy thing would be to run far far away and place yourself in a new environment with no expectations. For some people, this may even be a good step initially, but in the long run, you have to be your new self at home too.

In the diagram shown above, at one point you become a brother or sister to your parents, and you need to start acting like it. This means communicating about these expectations and speaking out the allowance to be different. That goes both ways. We often think our parents will never change, or they'll be set in their

ways forever. Truth is, everyone changes. If you give them room
to grow, they'll eventually do the same for you. At the same
time, I still think you need to speak out about how you're
changing. Talk about your hopes and priorities. Show your
family what's important to you through your actions. You should
also encourage them in what you see shifting in their lives
(especially your mom).

Also, as with every other issue to do with family, don't run
towards a new relationship because your family is holding the
past over your head. You have to go back to those relational
boundary stones and set them right. This will allow you to move
into new relationships with the right balance of the old you being
transformed and the new you free to keep changing. You'll also
lose that trendy effect, the one where you try to create a new
persona via style, music or whatever, to shake off the past.

4. Generational flow

Another lesson for me in taking on long-term commitments was
realizing I was part of a huge generational arc. I was in the
middle of my great-great-grandparents and my great-great-
grandchildren. I am the cause and effect of every one of their
choices, and every one of my choices will affect my children's
children... Whew!

My mother has always been great at
keeping us in touch with our past. She
works on genealogies, and gathers
histories and interesting anecdotes
about our family. She's kept things
alive that I would have easily forgotten
and therefore missed the relevance of
for my own life. We've noticed the
same thing in Heather's family as
they've written the story of their
international endeavors over five
generations. This creates such a great
perspective and helps you lose the
"I'm the center of the universe" delusion. This will also bring
some sobriety to your relational choices: If you like someone,
are you willing to have that attraction become your children's
children?

So as part of a centuries-old relational arc, we're being redeemed and healed and restored over time. Not just me, but the whole family. I won't get everything perfect in my lifetime, which is not a license for stupidity, but it helps me see my place in this longer redemption. The ripple effect of each choice will have a long-term result that I need to be aware of today.

5. I can't do relationships all by myself

Most of us would feel weird or just a little awkward bringing someone we like home to our family. Maybe because it's a loaded statement, like your mom will think this is it and start buying baby clothes. Or maybe you don't want your new friend to have a front-row view of all the dirty laundry. It could be that you like the exclusivity you've created and want to keep that romance in the dark. But whatever the reason is, we're missing something when our family is not the center of our new friendship. Because even at their worst (aside from abusive situations), families can be just the buffer you need to have a healthy place to form a great friendship. I know, even in the best of family relationships, bringing someone home to be part of that family can seem kinda advanced, like you're REALLY making a statement, like you want to marry them, and unless your family has known this person for years already, it's gonna seem awkward. But yeah, just get over it, because it's good for all of you.

I needed to be close to a family when I was getting to know Heather. Her family was great, but I was in a different city. So I sought out a very committed community to act as a kind of surrogate for the process. I don't recommend this, because it misses the point. Looking back, it would have been much better to spend a year hanging out with her family and mine, working a normal job and just learning to be natural around these people. Without this, I was kinda in a vacuum where I was the only reference for my own development.

Families provide a safe place to be together. Accountability when you get tempted. Great food and stuff to do that's more natural than contrived social scenes. They let your partner know where you've come from and who they may be connecting to in the long run. They can provide honesty, wisdom, and feedback, even the annoying kind. But I think the biggest benefit is the covering of the family. The term "chaperon" originally meant a hood or cap in late Middle English, something that gave protection. We need to realize that forming a relationship is a vulnerable thing. Trying to have a go on our own is not really smart. Until you form your own family, you are under the covering of your parents and to a lesser degree your siblings. This covering protects you from trying to be an adult before you're ready. Many people who date are trying to act like adults, like they're committed, when really, they have no clue about the future. So in the end, they're actually just playing around, which is why it's so easy for them to leave when they're tired of it all. Yeah, I'm a little upset at this. I see a lot of people hurting each other over and over again, acting the whole time like they know what they're doing. But they're terrified at the possibility of having their family involved in some meaningful way. This is a tell-tale sign that the root structure of the relationship is shaky. So use the family you have, crazy as it may be, to "cover" your development, because one day, wouldn't you want your son or daughter to do the same?

6. Families marry families

Eventually, you come to grips with the fact that your family will marry someone else's family. The sooner the better too, because if you realize this, you can get into that process right now. I said this earlier and I say it again: Marrying into Heather's family has been one of the smartest things I've ever done. Our families are really different. The diversity of Heather's family has created a lot of growth in my life (and some tension in theirs, sorry). My own family has added a lot to Heather's life and world view. The cross-cultural nature of our marriage has brought two completely different backgrounds into creative tension. And if two becoming one creates a third kind of entity, imagine what a whole tribe connected to another tribe creates.

Over the long term, the combination of these two families has been a tremendous blessing to us. They've added wisdom to our process, financial support and advice, joy in celebration, amazing food, history, and a sense of home... and it all keeps growing. I can't stress this enough: Two people were never meant to support a marriage alone. So the sooner you start thinking of relationships as extended families, the more whole the process becomes.

Imagine talking to your grandparents about their beginnings and bouncing your process off them. Or going to your new friend's extended family BBQ or Christmas celebration. Go ahead and dive into this, because even if you just stay friends with this person your whole life, you will have an amazing network of people who care for you, and you for them. It's completely worth it.

I think you get the point. If you overcome the weirdness of getting closer to family, you'll ground yourself in a much richer preparation. If you avoid the weirdness, your relationships will probably be kind of shallow. Some of you may have fantastic families where closeness would be the most natural thing in the world. Cool. But you may meet someone for whom this is not the case, so be sensitive in finding a way to make your relationship a family affair.

Finally, I just want to make a social comment. We've been kinda programed to be about the individual ("my personal Jesus" and "my Ikea castle"). But I've become convinced that God sees us as a tribe—a family—more than as an individual. I know that as a father my priority is the whole family. The individuals are important, but it's the tribe that's the most important. So when it comes to relationships, don't think of just the two of you as the goal. We marry from a family into another family and need every aspect of both of them.

Practice:

• *Track where you and your parents are on the first diagram. What can you do today (heart, communication, action, timing) to stay connected?*

• *How long would it take to bring restoration to the tricky parts of your family relationships, and can you hold on and stay connected when it gets even more complicated?*

• *Are you being allowed to change and are you giving room for others in your family to change as well? Are you holding anyone to expectations?*

• *In understanding your place in the generations, can you call your grandparents and ask them about their early years, priorities and values, and why they made the choices they did?*

• *How are you using your family as a covering and buffer in your present relationships? Are you getting closer to other families or just their daughters/sons?*

• *How would you like your kids and their friends to relate to your family in the future? Are you doing the same now?*

Seventeen.
Practicing in your neighborhood

Never doubt that a small group of thoughtful, committed citizens can change the world. Indeed, it is the only thing that ever has.
Margaret Mead

I need to start this chapter with a confession. I truly suck at being a good neighbor. I've been to 30 nations serving people I've never met, but I am terrified of going next door. I've given the last 27 years as a full-time volunteer to teach and train others, but I've never helped a neighbor's kid with their math homework (math is another thing I'm terrified of). I've risked my life feeding the homeless in Central America, but can hardly muster the courage to invite some strangers across the street for dinner. It's amazing how we can compartmentalize our lives like that, eh?

In fact, I think the problem of compartmentalization has been one of the main lessons of my life. I was expert at getting the pieces right while missing the whole. It was a lot easier to go to another country than to go across the street. It's risky business being known by other people and, by knowing them, becoming responsible. As long as I maintained "caring" as a compartment, it was something I could go do, and then come home and be safe. But in doing so, I was missing the bigger picture of relationships: community.

I think a lot of us escape into isolated relationships to be safe. Family and community is hard and they require responsibility. One-on-one is romantic, seemingly secure, and a lot more fun. But I've learned that if you want great relationships, you have to learn how to love your neighbor as yourself. It's where you learn the basic elements of love through seeing needs, acting on behalf of others, and using your creativity to solve problems. When you have these things down, you can bring them into your one-on-one relationship, which will also end up as a family, in a community.

Seeking the welfare of the city is seeking your own welfare
(Jeremiah 29). Caring for your neighborhood keeps the kids from
growing up and shooting you later. Picking up trash on your
street keeps other people from throwing out more. And if you're
not in a relationship right now and want to meet interesting
people, get out and meet basic needs.

I'm getting over my laziness and starting to get in touch with my
neighbors. I ran a cooking class recently and did some
photography for a neighbor's birthday party. I've been doing
some life coaching at local cafes and some training for local
artists. Starting next month, Heather and I will be managing
eight properties in our neighborhood as half business, half
community development project, all in an effort to stretch our
relational boundaries. See, when you're out using your gifts by
loving people you haven't chosen, you are developing a life,
your life. You're becoming a person with a rounded bunch of
abilities and passions, all being expressed in a caring way. This
love flowing through you meets your needs as discussed before,
but it also fulfills your identity (via the practice of your abilities),
which means you're not looking for something else to fulfill you.
You won't have your claws out in need of a distraction, because
your life will be filled with better things. In fact, in being a
community player, you may just bump into someone with a
similar heart with whom you can pick up trash, or whatever...

So let's get our foundations right. If we can't love our neighbor,
we'll go hunting for someone to love us. But if we find real
fulfillment in using our gifts to care for those around us, we're
already doing well and can only add to this with a special
someone, tee he he... This extroverted love is the best possible
grounding for your life in the real world because, despite all the
Hollywood versions of love, you will not live in an Italian
restaurant, dining by candlelight.

I'd like to make a few suggestions from Jeremiah 29 just to get
the ball rolling:

Build houses and settle down
The first connection to the community is home, having a place
where you're grounded and where you care about your street and
therefore your nation. You may not be able to buy a house right

now, but you need to make sure you are making wherever you are into a home. There is a restless spirit connected to people with no family and no place. Call it flexibility, but in the end it's a liability, because they're actually homeless, living in the circus (aka the city) rather than being established in a community.

You may be studying right now, or simply unsure about where you want to plant yourself. That's okay, just as long as you are making the most of each place you live in. Start with your room if that's all you have, and take good care of it. Then look outside and see how you can be a blessing to people in your neighborhood through hospitality or tutoring or caring for the elderly... If you see where you are as your home, you'll prepare yourself for the real deal later. This is in contrast to the idea of buying a house as an investment that you sell at the drop of an interest point.

Settling down seems like an anchor for a lot of people. And it's not because they have a better idea, it's that they have no idea and are afraid of missing something else. It's a kind of shopping spirit, the kind that hates to miss a sale or a better deal elsewhere. It's the fear of committing to something, because something else may be better. In the end, this spirit leads to a series of poor decisions, because there is no commitment to making wherever you are the best place it can be. The sooner you see settling as a positive thing, the sooner you can get on with your real life. Building and settling is a good thing and it creates good results.

Plant your vineyard
The next part is developing your work in the neighborhood or community. I think the best approach here is to find what you're best at and connect that with what the community really needs. I hear a lot of people talking about getting jobs or doing some deal where they can get a lot of money fast so they won't have to work any more than is absolutely necessary. This is a bad idea and creates all kinds of useless products and services based on meeting the person's needs, not the customers'. Your "vineyard" should be about something you love doing and genuinely want to share with others to sincerely help them. This kind of business lasts a long time and bears fruit for everyone.

My friends who started the cafe in an industrial area (where they also bought a home) are both very good at what they do and have started a little movement in the area of artists and workers who are trying to love God and do good. They create a sense of home, of space that people love being part of. It's like a community living room, where you feel safe and accepted. This is the best possible place to be relationally, because there's no weird agendas or vibes or cliques... I suggest you start or join something like this.

Get married[29]
The last part of God's instructions in Jeremiah is another form of commitment. Building is committing, settling is committing, planting is committing... see the theme? Learning to do community is learning to do commitment and it's commitment that we need to learn more than anything else. We get the romance and the dreams of something better, but what's generally missing in our models and our influences is commitment. Usually the only commitment we understand is the one to meet our needs. Marketers and film-makers milk this ad infinitum. But community isn't about me, it's about us.

> Marry and have sons and daughters; find wives for your sons and give your daughters in marriage, so that they too may have sons and daughters. Increase in number there; do not decrease. Also, seek the peace and prosperity of the city to which I have carried you into exile. Pray to the LORD for it, because if it prospers, you too will prosper. Jeremiah 29:6,7

And it's not like being married is the ultimate goal, like, if you get God, family, and community right, then you can have sex... It's simply a part of the next level of being "us". Have sons and daughters, raise them and see them married... and keep blessing the community so that you'll all do well. "For I know the thoughts I have for you," declares the LORD, "thoughts to prosper you and not to harm you, plans to give you hope and a

---

[29] Before I head into this section I just want to reiterate that marriage is not the ultimate relationship or THE goal. This section is really about commitment, and marriage is a solid way to show it, but the single committed life can be wonderful if it's an unconditional love you're showing to your family, community, and friends.

future" (verse 11). This is not a "Jesus loves you and has a plan for your life" deal. This is God blessing the community through you, because all of it is loved and thought of in terms of having a future and a hope. It's not about me doing well; it's all of us doing really well.

I may not have nailed this when I was younger, but I'm learning, and so are my kids. At 14 they were making skater videos and teaching their neighbors to make board games. At 15 they were in local craft fairs and cafes collaborating and making cool things to sell or give away. They're starting as young adults to integrate into their city via the neighborhood, and it's great to see, because they're spending their lives making music videos and children's books instead of chasing girls or boys. We have tons of people stay with us (we measure hospitality by the pound), my kids cook for them, take them on road trips, and genuinely love them. It's a beautiful thing.

Another beautiful thing is how this kind of community development is becoming such an organic and entrepreneurial lifestyle for some. In my travels, I keep coming across a lot of very cool people doing really natural and effective things. Some of my friends are working towards new business/cafe/ discipleship models in the Temple Bar district of Dublin, while others are forming artist communities in NYC. Each of these communities has distinct and creative ideas that people naturally hook up with and are drawn to. So if you can't start something, or you're "neighbor-retarded" like me, connect with other people who are doing great things. Most of the really good stuff is underground, so you'll have to dig a little and find the interesting goings-on. But put some effort in and you'll find some amazing people. Sometimes local churches are doing really good stuff, but from my experience, the great stuff is way under the radar, as it should be. Here's an interesting example I just pulled from my email 30 seconds ago (strange, eh?) from a friend who works at this place in Calgary. He just sent me their mission statement out of the blue:

> The House Coffee Sanctuary is a non-profit coffee shop owned and operated by First Alliance Church. Our doors opened in November 2001 with the purpose of being a positive influence in the Kensington community of

Calgary. As Christians, we believe we are called upon to reach out in love to our neighbors. We are about serving the community and building relationships. The House carries out its purpose through:
Serving fair-trade, organic coffee which ensures an improved quality of life in countries that rely on the coffee industry.
Supporting the artistic community through displaying local artwork and hosting local musicians on our stage.
Offering a variety of programs and events that meet the needs felt in the community, including a connection time for moms and pop culture videos & discussion groups.
We support and buy from a number of organizations with specialized causes; one of them is Cafe Femenino, a great foundation whose purpose is to empower women in farming.

Ah, drugs and good deeds do go together after all.

There are all kinds of things like this going on around the world, from Pirate Supply Store / kids tutoring centers in San Francisco (called 826 Valencia) to Graphic Designer / Rave communities in Lausanne and kiva.org (micro loans), which is a way to share the financial love around the world from the comfort of your laptop. So yeah, either start something like this or hook up with one. Get building, get planting, and get married.

By the way, if you are out there caring for people as a natural part of your life and are still not meeting others or don't have the time for relationships because you're so busy caring, then maybe you need to fine-tune that mission. Consider if you may have been compartmentalizing like me. Your caring, or at least a good part of it, should be neighborhood-based. Are you part of your community, working and living and shopping in the same place, or are you spread out over different communities? I find that in a compartmentalized life (work here, school there, church across town), we don't have the natural connections that form natural relationships.

Practice:

• *Do a quick audit of your life and map out where you work, study, eat, shop... then include where the people you love are (family, friends). How big is your map? How compartmentalized is your life?*

• *Do you consider where you are now to be home? What can you do to make it more of a home, even if it's temporary?*

• *If you're floating around now, what's the plan to get to the place where you would like to settle? Are you waiting for something?*

• *How can you integrate your life in a more natural cycle of involvement in a localized way?*

• *How are the pieces of your life allowing or hindering other people being a natural part of it?*

• *What are you doing to develop your abilities so that you have something to contribute to your community via the marketplace or whatever?*

• *Try to think past just being married to having a family that has families. How would you like all that to look in terms of location, work, creatively contributing to the community?*

• *How could that extended family bless the city or nation? What history would you like written about your family in 100 years?*

Eighteen.
Practicing with your best friends

If I had wings on my back I would fly to your side
And if there was something you lack, I would tell you a lie.
'Cause I want to give you everything...
I could pretend I'm enough to heal all your scars
And like a creator, I'd say I know just who you are
'Cause I want to be your everything...
But I'll always let you down
And I'll never be everything you need
But I can be loving you all the days that God gives us life
And if I had wings on my back I would fly to your side
Alli Rogers

I like how honest these lyrics are. They reveal the tension between our romantic hope (to be everything) and the reality of only being a part of someone's life. But really, being a part is wonderful. Earlier, we talked about how true and complete intimacy comes from a group, not an individual. Being part of that group in friendship is the most natural thing in the world. All the other stuff seems to be a kind of escape into an unreal world. Know what I mean?

I've said a bazillion times that a great relationship is built on unconditional love. And the best way I know to achieve that is by being an amazing friend, in a group of friends, connected to families. Being dedicated, creative, daring, and completely committed to the other person's well-being, with or without you in their future. Which means you have boundaries in the friendship so you don't send confusing messages. This is self-control. If you approach people like this, you're way less likely to rush into a "relationship". Instead, you'll have a lot of time to get to know them, which is a way of loving them by respecting their space.

Being an amazing friend
I don't want to be too prescriptive, but here's my fatherly advice about going from a place of meeting someone to maybe marrying them. It's a summary of the many ideas expressed in

this book—with some enhancements added—that are more intentionally about marriage. The first step is to create a sense of...

...*Trust:* After knowing someone for 20 years, if things get hard, it's trust that holds you together, or not. A lot of people remember how you started off with them. How fast you jumped into being physical, whether you messed around, how you kept their confidences. It's the cement at the base of your relational house, so you want to make it strong right at the beginning. This means that your number one priority is to be trustworthy. People cannot trust each other unless they have a basis on which to do so. It's unreasonable to say "just trust me" when they have no history. So when you get to know them, first impressions will be based on how trustworthy you are. And if you really like them, you need to be all the more careful not to move too fast. Just be faithful and consistent. This creates...

...*Safety:* If you single someone out and spend tons of time with them, you're giving the wrong impression. If you like them, make them feel safe around you. To develop a great friendship, they need to be brought into your circle (friends and family) and you into theirs. This sends the message that you're willing to be known, accountable, paced. You may feel like you'll lose them if you don't close the deal with some romantic pitch, but people are way more comfortable with a person who is caring but not overbearing. And if some other guy comes along and tells your friend how hot she is with her fiery red hair, and they end up dating, leaving you behind (at the cafe, reading Dylan Thomas, trying to figure out what went wrong), then at least you've loved them open-handedly. Here's a poem my daughter Jasmine wrote through a similar let-down. It's a parody on the theme:

Gruesome that be for I see
that fathomless fate that furiates
that Gruesome that is or shall or feign or hate
Me hate me it must or else
not for the likes could share TENDERNESS ONE THINKS
Nevertheless hearts must bleed
Hearts must bleed and beat and lust and cheat
or else bore away all that remains virtuous
in a gushing river of bloody disdain

Gruesome indeed, what else describes the war of deeds
and misdeeds that collides the separation of lovers
lovers of soul, spirit and mind...
mind that shows the heart where to sit in the folds of blindness
That my own love would die? For the love of itself?
Why be if not to satiate her own BEATING.
to satisfy the suckling lips that are its needs.
Be I worth this war, this pointless RED battle.
To tear me from mine and them from me?

Yeah.

Focusing on friendship first may make you nervous because you
really don't want to lose them. But I would ask you to consider
whether saying "I reaaally like you, don't like anyone else right
now, please?" is for your sake or theirs. Exercise some patience.
Maybe after that short ride in that jerk's flash car, your friend
with the fiery red hair may find that you were really much more
worth their time after all. Stick it out, my friend. It may be
painful, but better that pain than the other kind that comes from
rushing into a relationship for fear of losing someone. Pain isn't
a bad thing either; it helps us know what's really important and,
sometimes, truly loving someone will cost you.

Safety is created when you show a consistent love to all of your
friends. When you're doing really great things together instead
of, "what do you wanna do?" "I dunno, what do you wanna do?"
People can hang out these days like an Olympic sport but don't
necessarily create much or talk about important things. When
you go out, invite some of your other friends, even if it's three of
you. Learn to be community now, 'cause after you're married for
five years, it's that same community that will hold you together.
You'll have plenty of time to be just the two of you. And learn to
take some risks together. Instead of being alone in someone's
bedroom (a bad risk), go out and start a new business or try
running for a political office or meet some basic need in your
neighborhood (volunteer at a women's shelter or old folks'
home) together. This is...

...Creativity: If idle hands are the devil's workshop, then finding
something creative to do with your special someone(s) must be
blessed by angels. Heather and I cruised through Pacific islands

teaching in public schools and churches. Some friends of mine in Norway are meeting together as journalists and film-makers to see how they can influence their city over the next 20 years. Some other friends are rescuing dying babies from hospitals in Uganda (caring for over 100 at a time); they just went out and made it happen. This sort of stuff will clear your head really fast. You'll be so busy loving people, you won't have any time to date them.

I think this kind of foundation is also the best way to meet other people with like interests. Find what you're super passionate about, get some training, and then get busy developing your skills. People will get to see the real you, both in difficult situations and at your best. This is so much better than fronting in lame social scenes, trying to impress or get someone's approval. For me and Heather, and a bunch of other friends at the time, this really simplified our relationship. We had a lot of cool things going on and this helped us pace the friendship.

Being a friend is all you need for quite a while, and it has none of the complications of dating. In fact, I can't think of one good thing you get by dating someone that you can't have by being a great friend. Unless you think tongue-lunging will help you understand them better? Some people do; they're like, "I need to really see if I could be with this person the rest of my life, and I can only know that by being, ya know, physical". How shallow is that? That you can't really get to know a person without taking something you're not committed to following through with. I think it's weak and cruel. And did I mention stupid? 'Cause the number of times you have to go through this, and the number of people that get hurt along the way, is really insane. There has to be a better way, and friendship is that way. It may sound a little prudish for your fluttering heart, but over time, I think you'll find that while emotions come and go, committed friends last a lifetime. And if that's too hard for you, sit down with a bunch of people in their late 20s and see how dating is working out for them.

Attractions
In Chapter Two we looked at all the different kinds of attractions and how cool but also confusing they are. If you're just getting

to know someone (uninformed optimism) and are starting to
have a lot of feelings for them, I suggest you do the following.

1. Don't tell them, or your friends. If you're not ready to change
   your life and live with them for the next 60 years, then they
   don't need to know how your hormones or neurons are doing.
   Not yet anyway. By speaking out how you feel, you are
   creating a pseudo relationship. One that exists on a chemical-
   emotional level but not realistically on any other level. You
   don't know them (their identity, values, family, future) and
   they don't know you. You may have had some great
   conversations so far, but all that means is that you've had
   good conversation. If you can maintain this for a year or two,
   you may have something. During that time you can encourage
   them and make some room in your life for them, but don't tell
   them how you feel just yet. Remember what happened the last
   time you told someone too early?

2. Tell God. And maybe your dad or a father figure if you have
   that kind of relationship (nothing against moms here, it's just
   that they tend to be more accepting than dads). Telling God
   allows you to ventilate your heart (because you do have to
   relieve the pressure, otherwise you'll blurt something out
   before it's time). You can tell God how much you like them
   and why, in detail. This not only gives vent to your feelings,
   but now you are talking to *their Father*, which tends to purify
   the attraction. It helps you see them from God's perspective,
   which creates more respect and puts a healthy check and
   balance into the chaotic mix of attractions.

3. If you take your time to really get to know them, you'll start
   to see past the façade of typical attractions to the real person.
   Their personality will unfold as they can trust you more. Their
   character will be exposed (the good and the bad), which will
   either become even more attractive or make you think twice
   about what you first thought you saw. Not that this should
   hinder the friendship, but it puts the whole thing into
   perspective. What I've found is that if I give people time to be
   themselves, I discover whole new levels of attraction.

4. Remember the line, "I love me, I want you"? This is
   ultimately what dealing with attractions is all about. Learning

to love them and not yourself through them. This takes self-control. If you really like them, what's the best course of action for them? What's the best timing, the best way to treat them, the right amount of time together... for them? If you think blurting out how much you like them is the best thing for them, then fine, but be careful and check your heart first. If you can't use self-control over expressing attractions, you sure as hell won't be able to control yourself when it comes to getting physical. Faithful with little, faithful with much.

I've had the privilege of meeting and becoming friends with a lot of people over the years. Each one of these people is attractive to me in different ways and for all kinds of reasons. If I considered each attraction as an indicator that my love for Heather was waning or wasn't real any more, I'd be psychotic. The reality is that you'll have attractions for the rest of your life. There's a lot of beauty and wonder in the world and you need to learn to appreciate it in its place.

I just got back from a trip to Norway, which happens to be a country full of wealthy, intelligent, amazingly gorgeous people with perfect skin...everywhere! It's kinda strange actually. I mean, really, that many people with great skin in one place? Is it the herring? Anyway, super attractive, right? So what I do is take a series of portraits (now on Facebook) and, under each one, I list some wonderful identity attributes I saw. This is honoring the attraction with an appropriate expression, instead of dumping the fam and going for the red sports car and the new (blonde-haired perfect-complexioned) girl.

Don't torpedo a budding friendship by assuming your feelings mean this is it! If this person is special to you, act that way in all the other things we've talked about and then share your feelings in the right...

...Timing

Timing is a form of self-control. Get it right in the beginning and you'll set foundations for the rest of your life. Rush into it now and you'll probably be saying goodbye within the year. What you're looking for instead is a healthy cycle. And while I can't predict what that means for each person, I've found that a year or two is a good timeframe to get to know someone to the point where you may want to commit yourself to them for the rest of your life.

The first few months is that "uninformed optimism" phase. When you think they're amazing, because what you see may be really awesome, but you only see a little. Don't talk about feelings or make commitments when you need the time instead to get to know them and to be known for who you are. If you rush in now, you'll spend all your time putting energy into the façade, the impression you want to keep making on someone. Eventually you turn into someone else, because you can't be yourself after fronting for that long. Friends don't have to act like anything for approval; this first three months should be about just being yourselves and giving each other the room you need to develop your creativity and the other cool things in your life. And by the way, if there aren't other cool things in your life, be very careful, 'cause you may just be looking for someone to "save you".

The second few months grows into the "informed pessimism" phase. Now you know them a little better and the warts are clearer. No prob for a friend though, right? And maybe because they didn't have to perform for you, you actually like the real them a little better, and they you. A lot of people check out at this phase cause their hopes are dashed (the idea of you they built up in their heads). Pity, cause there's not a relationship on the planet that doesn't need the reality of disappointment to create a stronger bond. This is where you learn to be committed despite what you may or may not get out of the relationship. It's a time to test the real selfishness that comes out when everything isn't as we'd like it. It's probably the most important part of developing a friendship, because if you stick with people during these seasons, you have friends for life, whether you marry them or not.

The third few months is when you come into "hopeful realism". You've had some history, some time to see them in a lot of different contexts, and time to see how they handle conflict or pressure. And however they've acted, you now know them or at least you're starting to get a real feel for who they are. If you have a long-distance friendship, you may need even more time to see if your values line up, because values have to be observed and not just texted back and forth. If through all this time you've kept your feelings to yourself, there is no crushing disappointment if you discover that this may not work out as you initially thought. There will still be expectations that have to be dealt with, because whether you share attractions or not, people will build expectations in their hearts. And this will be disappointing for one if not both of you. But this is way more manageable than setting someone up by alluding to love but not really following through on it. This is why keeping this person's heart safe and doing good works together are an important buffer so the other person isn't led along a path you can't stick to. On the other hand, if you have had the time to see that your values and futures could line up, and you are willing to commit to them, then you can move forward with confidence.

The fourth season (now a year, or year and a half) moves you into a place of "informed optimism". At this stage, you should know the other person's family, and they should know yours. You'll know as much as you need to know about the other person to decide what you want to do about the relationship. You've given them time to be themselves, you've seen how they handle money and kids and their family, and you've had time to show your values in all these areas. Now it's just a matter of either commitment to marriage or life-long friendship. In either case, you'll have been honorable towards them and able to develop a level of intimacy you can maintain, marriage or not. I have a few friends like this, people I've known for decades who are super close and are part of the overall intimacy in my life, but I'm only married to one. So I would encourage you to develop a few friendships that keep you from getting top heavy on one person unless you know you want to marry them. A lot of people struggle with this idea because they feel like they can't really get to know someone unless they have an exclusive relationship with them. Okay, but for every three or four exclusive relationships people tend to have, only one may work out, and the other three end up in pain, as in, you would not like to meet them on the street. I don't think the system is working, so why not try to develop a group of non-exclusive friendships until you get to the point of wanting to really commit to someone (as in, put a ring on their finger).

Note: I need to mention here that it's nearly impossible to follow through on these ideas if you're the only one trying. One of the reasons I advise developing a group of friends is that we all need to be on the same page. We need to revolutionize how we relate to each other. We need to stop all the lame innuendo about why this person went out with that person, and "did you hear that that person likes so and so?" Honestly, are we not old enough and human enough to develop a better way to be friends? If you could share these ideas, over a BBQ or coffee together with your closest friends, then maybe you could all be safer and more creative and caring over a longer period of time, without all the pubescent activity that passes for "relationships".

The main thing about timing is to give all of you the space to develop your identity, values, and plans for the future. You don't want to marry someone who doesn't know these things about themselves, and you're not ready to be married if you're still figuring this out for yourself. So don't go telling someone you love them and think they're right for you when you haven't got a clue about the next few years. One day you or they will finally wake up to who they really are and say "why are we doing this? why are we living in this country? AND WHY ARE YOU IN MY BED?" It gets really ugly when people finally figure out their identities but realize they've married someone who doesn't get them or share their core values. And by values I mean if you want children and how many, if you are an international or a local bod, how you deal with money, roles in the home, aging parents... These are the things you have to figure out before you make commitments, and this is why timing is so crucial. Give yourself space to grow up. I mean, don't take forever, but start working on this more seriously. Maybe if you weren't dating so much, you'd have more time to develop yourself. Was that mean?

Commitment
Okay, so now it's down to the wire. If you're following the suggestions above, a natural season of readiness will emerge. Even if you really like a few people, the clarity about identity and values will probably tip one of these people over the top of your scales. All you need to know at this point is that your known values and identity will not drive them crazy and they will not annoy you with theirs (knowingly at least) for the rest of your lives. And then you have to decide: Will I commit to this

person? Your feelings will change over the years, but will you commit to them? Their appearance will change over the years, and some of their priorities or sense of humor, but will you commit to them? They are no more perfect than you are, so will you commit to them? After all the seasons I mentioned above, and all the care and development of friendship and creativity, it comes down to a simple choice: Will I *create love* with this person? Do I choose to be an amazing friend for the rest of their life, with all our shortcomings, and knowing that they cannot "complete me"? Will I *be* love to them?

I want to emphasize here that commitment is one of the central tenets of unconditional love. It means the world to God and to each other. It has to be taken super seriously and will have eternal results (such as new people: children). So your "yes" must be "yes", or your "no" should be "no". Which is why I keep harping on the fact that we should not share attractions too soon and jump into things we're not ready to follow up on, because when we do, our "yes" becomes "maybe" and then the broken commitments mount up until our "yes" becomes shallow and worthless. If you know this now, then you'll have the strength and the guts to love someone over time, and your communi-cation and actions will be consistent and appropriate. And all the while you will be telling that guy or girl, "you can trust me; my 'yes' means 'yes', I will never lead you on or defraud you, and when I say 'I love you', I will mean it as long as we live".

Now this final commitment may come at the end of a long and healthy friendship, but I think wherever you are in this process, you can start getting ready for this today. In fact, I suggest you pick a year when you want to be married and start asking:
- *What do I need to be working on right now so that in a year or two I'm ready to make that kind of commitment?*
- *How am I relating with my friends today? Am I creating safety and cool projects to work on so that we're buffering our time with good stuff?*
- *Where have I created weirdness in other relationships and how can I apologize for that and make it right, creating a better friendship along the way?*
- *Do I have a life, one that I'd love to share with someone, and if not, what do I need to do to get back on track with my own development?*

Lose the myths

Finally (and I mean finally—sorry for being so hard at times; call it tough love from a dad who cares, 'cause I really do), it's my hope that in learning to love God, our families, friends, and neighbors in unconditional ways, we'll dethrone the selfish myths of "love languages" and being "captivating" enough for others to notice us. I hope that we'll revolutionize the relational norms of culture with something amazing from God, that love moving through us freely to others will meet our needs and have a transformational effect on the ones we love (including our cities).

To be fair, I think people do have love languages, but focusing on them just isn't helpful. I think people are captivating, but focusing on how worthy you are can take your eye off the ball. Overall, the literature on relationships today, especially the Christian stuff, is very self-centered. And this is tricky, because it's true that if you don't know and love yourself, you can't love your neighbor—or your spouse. But there's a cult of self that's been forming around this stuff since the '60s, and it's missing the paradox: that we die to live, we give to receive, and in being patient and kind and bearing all things we find a love much more powerful than the one we were dying to get.

This cult of self has created a kind of mysticism that makes God into the Great Puppeteer, manipulating people's choices and feelings so that He can deliver "the one" for *me*, or in the right time "show me the one". We can actually think God has someone for us, designed for us, like from an assembly line, or at best, that He's match-making because He knows us and loves us. I think God does love us and it's for this reason that He doesn't bring people together. The love of God is expressed *in the process, the lessons, and the opportunities* we have to love our families and neighbors. The wisdom of God is to *teach us unconditional love* so we can create it and give it away. If God delivers people to me, there's no learning, no giving, and therefore no real love. This "pray for your mate" idea is not based on how God really works with us, but rather on our fear, our laziness, and our fatherlessness. It's a void we are trying to fill by creating God in the image of our need. It's called idolatry.

Now I may have got you all this way kinda liking me... and then stuck my foot in it at the very end. But I gotta risk this. Having a wrong view of our Creator will mess with your whole life. If we're truly fatherless, let's acknowledge it and get to know God as parent. If we're afraid, then let's ask for help with our fear. If we're really lazy, then let's work on the real issues and find the wisdom of God to figure it out. Better this than to have a misguided approach to one of the most important issues of our lives and times. God is a wonderful friend, coach, and mother-father when it comes to relationships, but waiting around for the Creator of the universe to do all the work will only lead to relational weirdness, as in "God told me to marry you". Which has happened, like three recorded times in 3,500 years, but it's not the norm. The norm is to walk in the ways of God, learning to create love, and it's in this hope that these ideas and principles will be a blessing to you and your children's children.

Nineteen. A letter to Jordan

...Grant that I may not so much seek
to be consoled as to console;
to be understood, as to understand,
to be loved as to love;
Francis of Assisi

My son Jordan had just turned 18 and had the wonderful opportunity to work on the feature film *10,000 BC* while they were shooting in Namibia. He had flown there from NZ full of excitement to continue his homemade education as a director. A couple of my dear friends had taken him on the project but warned me that being on a film set was not always a pretty picture. It was common for a lot of people to hook up while working together and use sex as a distraction or self-promotion. In light of this, I guess all the gambling and drinking wouldn't be that bad? Anyway, Jordan had been writing to me about all his observations, opportunities, and the situations he'd gotten into. They were pretty colorful and inspired my father's heart to write the following letter:

Dear Jordan
A friend of mine wrote a couple of days ago to tell me that he
had sex with his girlfriend. It wasn't the term he used. He
sanitized it a little by saying that he had gone too far with girls
recently and then way too far, or all the way...

I was thinking about this and what struck me was that we
"know", in very general terms, that this is wrong for a hundred
reasons, and if pushed, we could recite some of the reasons. But
we keep the general "wrongness" of the thing in the back of our
minds. Back there with the other generalities of being a
Christian.

For the most part, they're safe there. Most people never have
overt sexual opportunities to challenge these generalities out of
their hiding place. "Knowing" sex before marriage is wrong is a
tidy position that's easily challenged by the physical reality of
someone sitting right in front of you (or on top) who's ready and
willing. In this position, the thoughts alone will not defend you.

When the real challenge hits us, we're often unprepared or out of practice because we're mentally and spiritually out of shape. Sexuality moves from a mental possibility to a physical reality in a few milliseconds. The sheer strength of temptation rushes past those 100 reasons of why this is a bad idea as though they were blurred posters on a subway route. In the hot seat, your values don't make any sense, because your senses are busy.

Before you could reasonably articulate just one good reason why you should put the brakes on, a million other processes have already kicked into their natural state. Blood flows to the extremities, emotions bounce around the heart and mind, beauty waves its amazing wand and within moments, you have broken God's heart and later, each other's.

Afterwards you have depression or justification... and the trail begins again. The guilt of blowing it takes you two steps back relationally, and it's this added stress which makes you even more relationally vulnerable next time. The problem is that most people keep exercising all the wrong faculties and so are just as vulnerable in the future because all they walk away with, was that it was all wrong. The very thing they already knew.

So my son, the reason I am writing to you, on a film set, with a hundred very real possibilities to engage in very natural but untimely sex is this; I want you to keep exercising the right things in the right way.

Love is not selfish. *Keep loving people in the right way. Yes, this will draw them closer to you and make you even more attractive. But for your part, when you see the line getting crossed (and you'll see it way before someone is ever on top of you), love them enough to clarify the line. It's a line of respect, of space and domain. It's theirs, not yours and even when they want to give it up, clear communication reminds them that there is something better.*

Provision is what you give from your abundance and from what God is giving you. *Are you feeling it? Do they? Are you calling it down and allowing it to flow through you? If so, this is your security. This intimate provision is the stuff that keeps your space intact because you will not be needy. If those around you*

*are needy, you know what their real need is and what its
fulfillment will look like.*

***Value is knowing your soul is more valuable than the whole
earth.*** *The same for the girl right next to you. Practice the
respect of this value. Practice calling out the value through
detailed and thoughtful encouragement. Cherish the value in the
care of your person and of those around you through servanthood. If someone is tempted to give themselves to you
prematurely, know clearly that they are sacrificing their value
and willing to steal yours. Not cool and easily rejected if your
value fitness is intact.*

***Destiny is your future and your hope of all the good things you
get to create.*** *Your sexual future is about your future family and
it's a wonderful thing. It needs to be cherished and protected.
You exercise this by dreaming it, planning for it, talking about it.
Making it real through the spoken word so that when another
word, or spoken challenge asks to defraud that destiny, you're
already busy thank you very much.*

*Jordan, I know you understand these things for the most part.
Having eternity in our hearts, I think everyone understands these
things. I speak them out because these very foundations move
from the forefront of a fit heart and mind to the back of the line
in a busy world. An unloving world. A needy world.*

*Stay fit my son.
with love
Dad*

Jordan went into the desert with a very clear ambition about who
he was and what he wanted to create. He was struck by the talent
and commitment of the people he was working with, and grew in
love with them as the days and weeks passed. When the makeup
crew (one of the departments he worked with) pooled all their
per diem (cash they got for food each day) to give him a gift
because he wasn't getting paid, he took the same amount and
bought all of them Lindt chocolates which they found at their
stations the next day. When some people were having a little too
much to drink at the end of the hard shooting days, Jordan would

go into the pubs and take girls home, one by one, getting them safely back to their apartments.

He was so clear about what he wanted, and was so engaged in something he loved, that people didn't want to mess with that. He's an attractive guy with a lot of potential, and yet no one propositioned him or, as he puts it, "evil didn't find me". When you have a clear eye and a sense of place and destiny, you won't be distracted by lesser things. Instead, you'll have something wonderful to give.

Stuff I did learn from my dad
I really wish this had been my experience growing up. It would've been wonderful to have had this kind of encourage-ment and support while I was trying to figure out how to live in a difficult world. Fortunately, I had God to re-parent me and it turned out pretty well. One of the reasons was that I was able to build on the things my father *did do* for us, and the things he *did teach* us. He was a super hard worker and a faithful provider. This (along with my mom's unconditional love) gave me a decent basis of security, or at least enough to build on as an adult. As my father grew older, he grew softer, more in touch with his artistic nature, and he became a better communicator.

As I started to process my adult life and the issues that came up, I would often write to him and share what I was learning. He really couldn't respond in the beginning (due to his guilt of leaving and the rejection he felt), but as time passed, he started writing back. After 15 years, we were fully reconciled and communicating fairly regularly. What this taught me was that relationships take time and that everyone changes. Even in his absence, I was learning from the things he suffered as well as from the mistakes he'd made. But in closing, I want to acknowledge that while he didn't do his best, he did love us by the sweat of his brow and the maturing process he went through.

At the end of the day, our commitment to God and our family will teach us, if we're willing to learn and apply those lessons. Even in difficult and dysfunctional situations, there's grace, because over time you can turn the tide of your own life by making wise and caring choices. As Heather and I prepare for our 25th anniversary, I feel like I'm turning the tide of divorce and broken commitments from generations by staying plugged in each and every day. I am changing the nature of our family's relationships by investing in my kids and their identities, their relationships and their futures.

As I've said so many times, I guess it comes down to taking our attention away from being loved and putting it into loving others. A lot of people seem to be looking for someone amazing or beautiful to love them. It's like winning the lottery. But loving other people is something anyone can do, immediately. No super model or super anything required. Why chase the advertised fantasy when you can create something real, right now. You can do this, today, by calling your dad... And then call a friend to go out with you and staff a city mission project or whatever you can do to give something of yourself, your time, your creativity, your heart. Anyone can do this, but not everyone does, and this is our problem. I write this with the hope that you will be part of the solution.

Benediction
So may you find a worthy challenge for your gifts and abilities. You've been so blessed with all kinds of potential and all kinds of ways to love people around you. May you have a heart for your neighborhood and develop amazing friendships there. Take some risks to love those not being loved, stretch yourself in being generous. And may you create a great love for people, so that you rise above the games being played around you. Talk with your friends about how you'd like to form a safe and caring intimacy amongst yourselves. May God, your family, and your true friends join forces to create a new culture of relationships, so that anyone who's lucky enough to cross your path will be blessed by the amazing love you show for each another.

I know I've laid out a lot of challenges to you, and some of it may seem super hard, especially if you feel a huge deficit in your heart. But it's in this very place of need that you're most ready to love. It's the sensitivity to pain that allows you to feel and minister to the hurts of others. It's in the silence of people not encouraging you that you can hear the cry of others and their need for encouragement. It's in the lack of understanding of your future that you can join up with others who need something better to do with their lives. Like Francis of Assisi, ask God to assist your soul in being more about other people than about yourself. If you take this challenge, you'll enter a space that's so amazing and deep, you'll know the love of God moving through you, which is all we really need. Everything else will be icing.

Written with the love of a father.
Patrick Dodson
July 2009

Appendix 1:
Rip this out for your journal...

"Must, kiss, arghh, her..., no, wait, what's next?"

I wanted to put all the pieces together as a simple outline in case it's helpful or as a reminder when the neurotransmitters kick in.

- *start with loving your family; it's your training ground, or it's baggage you'll carry anyway, so work on it now*
- *learn to be an amazing friend, listening, trustworthy, committed, supportive, facilitating, creative together...*
- *love the neighborhood, meet basic needs*
- *develop faithfulness and pace yourself, take your time (remember the four stages)*
- *lose the list, manage attractions and don't make decisions based on them*
- *let time knead the relationship*
- *be honest about needs; are yours being met by God and family or are you looking for her or him to save you? if so, pace yourself and don't use them*
- *love the neighborhood, meet basic needs*
- *develop a clear sense of value (identity) and destiny (future plans)*
- *articulate your values, listen to theirs (kids? money? roles? place to live? care of elderly parents?)*
- *hang out with your families (yours and theirs); friends are okay, but they often don't work the deep stuff*
- *consider (not in fear, but in wisdom) the long-term implications of your values working out together*
- *love the neighborhood, meet basic needs*
- *make a commitment and stick to it*
- *when it gets hard, read the book again; it will get hard*
- *when it's going well, celebrate but don't measure your relationship by this; you're both growing up and the relationship is there to facilitate the process*
- *don't be selfish, ever; have kids or adopt or just find some to care for, and remember that the more you give away, the more flows through you; your benefit is that you become a loving person, a rarity in the world today*
- *depend on the wider family; we can't do love by ourselves*
- *love the neighborhood, meet basic needs*

Appendix 2:
Some questions from my friends

I get a lot of questions about the way I present relationships. Some people ask if dating is okay or not, others, about the boundaries of being physical. My approach is not to tell people how and when to relate, but to look at unconditional love as the foundation that tends to build better friendships in the long run. The rest takes care of itself for the most part. So please don't move past the important stuff (like the first few chapters) and look for some clever or religious way to get what you want out of someone else.

I really appreciate the conversations and questions I get, because not only do we need to process out loud, I learn tons from the feedback. I'm sorry I can't process with you directly, but I've gathered some questions from five of my friends (names changed to avoid international embarrassment) covering most of the typical topics, which I'll share below. I'll also be setting up a site (www.patrickdodson.net/relationships) to create a public forum for discussion, so you can express your ideas and questions as well as hook your friends into a conversation that may benefit the whole group. Until then, here's a short Q & A:

Attractions and emotions:
Maria: If attractions aren't a leading indicator for getting into a relationship, why are they so stinking strong?

Yeah, good question. It's amazing how persuasive feelings can be, especially the ones that kick in the dopamine. Two ways to look at this. One is that God or evolution has wired us to find a mate via the feelings. The problem with this is that after you've found a mate, you still have strong attractions for others. So that can't be the answer. The other way to view it is that the strength of the feelings is simply a wonderful part of being human. They're like spices, strong spices, and you take them for what they are, strong feelings in a certain space and time, but you don't add meaning to them. All they mean is that you like something about someone. It will change, shift to others, and ebb and flow like the ocean. If you don't add meaning to it, then you

can enjoy the attraction and simply add it to a bigger process
which involves values, and goals, and timin¿ ..

*Nathan: The last few days I have been feeling like my emotions
for her are gone. Before that I was ve ʼ excited about everything,
and now it feels so different. I talked with her this evening, and
that rekindled it a bit. But I still don't understand how things can
change so fast.*

Your feelings are not meant to guide you. How you feel for her is
not an indicator at all, except to show that emotions are both
fickle and wonderful. That's pretty much it. Don't give them too
much credit. You're not basing your choice for her on how you
feel; it's whether you want to love her or not.

*Nathan: So I should base my choice on wanting to love her or
not, not on feelings? Anything else more specific?*

1. That's right. 2. Do you want to love her? How? How can you
serve and bless her? Do your values line up (*see below*)? If you
start looking for indicators (how she looks, makes you feel,
cooks...) you'll miss how wonderful she really is. Just let the
friendship grow, and be patient.

*Nathan: But do you think that emotions and attractions need to
be there at all?*

I wouldn't start a friendship based on attractions, so no, they
don't need to be there. As the friendship develops, a lot of people
look for attractions to lead them further. Okay, that's one
criterion, but it's so dodgy I wouldn't give it much credit. One of
my friends had a great thing going with someone until her
"mentor" asked if she was passionate about him ("because you
can't marry someone you're not passionate about", they said).
She wasn't at the time and so she cut off the relationship.
Weirdness, and unnecessary. If you need to feel something
strongly before committing, then ask yourself why and if that's
how you want to make life decisions.

Finally, you will feel for a person you get close to. If you're a
great friend and loving them unconditionally, you'll probably

have all kinds of emotions kick in. I'm just saying you don't need them there at the start.

Alex: It can't be all unconditional love, can it? After all, there has to be something that attracts you to this one person more than everybody else? Are you saying values alone are enough to commit to someone?

Values are huge, but the point is that attraction has to be dethroned. People who place it high on their list are looking for something rather than being something for others. It's a lousy foundation that eventually undermines you or at least makes you more miserable than you need to be. Why does there have to be something that draws you? I understand that that's cool, but it still sounds like you want something. Bad way to start.

Alex: I always thought both values and attraction should be there. That it could help you single out a few instead of running after everybody. And then you focus on being something for that person. Why did God make us this way, that we get attracted, if it's of such little value? I thought it was to help us choose somebody more easily? And I don't mean attraction = looks only, but also personality, humor, a general connection... but still not right?

No, that's cool. I think attractions are a gift from God too. Do they help us narrow the field? I'm not sure. I've found that I'm attracted to people all the time. And for all the reasons you've mentioned. But over the years you learn that attractions are a moving target. You may really like someone for a few months, and then it's gone. Or you get attracted, get married and then get attracted to someone else. So what do you do with the new attraction? I'm just saying they're not a huge indicator and that people put too much emphasis on them. I think values are a much better way to "narrow the field" because they don't shift, while feelings change like the weather.

Nathan: I found this quote in a book: "Mild attraction and desire coupled with other areas of compatibility and friendship is healthy, because most of your time together in marriage is actually nonsexual." Any comments?

The comment is true about sexuality; for most married couples it's apparently once a week. But are mild attraction and desire constants? Probably not. These things come and go all the time. Attraction and desire are good, just not a sign of compatibility or even a healthy relationship. In fact, I'm not sure "compatibility" is a healthy term—more Darwinian really. I think the selfish approach to knowing someone (Do I like them? Am I attracted to them? Do I enjoy being with them?) limits friendships. There may be people who would be wonderful to know, but we write them off because they don't meet our criteria. Jesus looked at potential, the soul, the stuff that takes time to see. I'm just saying that if you pursue people for them and not for you, you'll see even more attractive things, you'll enjoy being with them, and that *creates* desire. In this way, you create a deeper friendship based on commitment to them and all the various layers of who they are.

Maria: Would you call emotional intimacy a need? Isn't that something we all need? Wouldn't that be part of a healthy relationship?

Yes, we need intimacy. The question is, how do you develop it? If you're only looking to receive it, you become an empty well and your partner will never be able to fill you up. Intimacy is something we give, and in the giving we receive.

Just friends...
Alex: I think it would be weird in our culture not to date, and not say that you like a girl. Can't you date without the complexities of expectations or getting too physical?

I know what I'm suggesting is not typical. What is typical is that we have a super high failure rate in dating and marriage, so I think we need a bit of a revolution. People rush into dating based on feelings and attractions, all of which change over time. What I'm saying is we should learn what friendship is about and not use language we don't really understand or mean, not until we've had enough time with someone and we're ready to commit to them. Plus, it's super hard to be in a "relationship" and not create expectations or get too physical. When you're close to someone, being physical is the most natural thing in the world; the question is if it's the right time or not, and unless you're married, it's not the right time. Why do that to each other when you could be good friends anyway? As I've said, I can't see any advantage to dating that you can't get as a good friend.

Maria: *Would you say it's selfish to just enjoy being with somebody?*

No. I think it's wonderful to be with people you like for any given reason. But if you make this a prerequisite (so you only hang out with people you enjoy), then your foundation is about you. So you won't have friends, just potential dates.

Nathan: *I've been keeping in touch with someone and we've got to know each other better, and I feel like things are pointing more and more in the direction of having a "relationship" which I think is good. What do you think?*

Madeline L'Engle says she doesn't like the term "relationship" because that always seems to end up in bed. She prefers "love" and "friendship". I couldn't agree more. Whenever we talk about creating a "relationship", we seem to enter that weird third space that just turns so unnecessarily dramatic. I would encourage you to define what an amazing friendship could be like, without the idea of dating or being in a so-called relationship. What are the Godly values of friendship and how could you walk that out with her and others at the same time? Get to know your identity and values, express them, and listen to hers. Over time, this may lead to a commitment, but even if it doesn't, everything you do with her should build towards a friendship you can keep the rest of your lives whether you get married or not. Just don't do anything you'd regret or be embarrassed about later.

John: *How do you remain good friends with someone of the opposite sex at a distance? In a way it seems like "being in a relationship" would give the friendship some sort of structure. It seems harder to just be friends and not have expectations, because eventually there are expectations put on the two of you by others who don't understand why you're not dating...*

If you gotta call something a "relationship" just to keep pursuing or be pursued, then it's a sign that you haven't got the basics of

friendship in place (in other words, you're rushing it). Here's
what you could do instead:
  • develop an interest in the other person's well-being and
    what's best for them (encourage them to move forward, even
    if that means to a different location without you)
  • be committed to knowing them in depth (distance is not an
    issue—internet)
  • commit to a wide-ranging group of people that you're
    befriending, which shows you are not trying to suck the life
    out of one person by isolating them
You never have to date to avoid people misunderstanding you.
Just ignore those people. Liking someone is fine, wanting to
speak it out is pretty normal, but doing so, as you've already
seen in the past, is not helpful. Distance will not take anything
away from a friendship. A lot of people get nervous about losing
someone (like they ever had them), so they try to lock in the deal
with the schmooz. It's kinda weak really.

Helen: So what do you think about kissing before marriage?

Well, here's a question: Why is it okay to kiss someone you're
not fully committed to, like in a dating relationship, but it's not
okay to kiss other people once you're married? It's because when
you're married, you're committed, right? So when you're not
married, you're not committed and you can kiss a lot of different
people, because you're not committed to them... But if you're
not committed to them, why are you kissing them?

One reason is that you feel like it. And the feeling is really
important, because it means you "love them", right? And if you
love them, surely you can kiss them? But maybe you don't love
them. Maybe you're kissing them because you like it. Most
people don't figure out how to truly love someone until after
they've had years together. Most people kiss simply because it
feels good, or they don't want the guy to date someone else. So
be honest with yourself. Most guys will be your friend so they
can kiss you (or more), and most girls allow themselves to be
kissed so they can be the guy's friend. In both cases, it's leverage
and pretty selfish. If it's truly love, then respect and timing
would be at the top of your priorities.

Another way to look at it is how you would want your kids to be when they're your age. Would you be okay with some guy kissing your daughter in a dating scenario? I wouldn't recommend kissing, because you don't deserve to kiss someone you're not 100% committed to. And partial commitment doesn't count.

Women leading the relationship?
Maria: I'm tired of waiting for him to say something, but I feel awkward about "leading" the relationship, or even initiating.

I hear you. Most guys are way too nonchalant in their communication. Some of them are playing the field and others are simply not paying attention. From my perspective, most guys are just plain retarded when it comes to relationships. I'm not name-calling here; I mean our growth has been literally stunted by not having dads that have modeled, discussed, and developed relational skills with us. In this case, I think women need to help us understand what's going on. Some have gone so far as to say that women actually "civilize" men by teaching them relational skills. I can take that, and honestly, I learn so much from the women in my life that I have no problem with a women leading various aspects of the friendship.

If you look at your probable strengths as a woman—intuition, relational orientation, communication skills, strong familial commitment, good sense of timing—you are totally equipped to lead relationally. These are things we as men can learn from you. Plus, it's kind of insane to wait around for us to initiate out of our weakness. So don't be shy with your strengths. Most guys are not put off by a woman who knows things he doesn't. If they are, it's not your problem.

Andrea: Where are the real men? Seems like everyone I know is a boy.

Most of the real men are married, because that marriage *made* them into something solid. What you have to work with (before marriage) is boys trying to grow up in a vacuum. Some of these guys are so far from reality (in general) that they're spending 1,500 man-years per day on World of Warcraft (that's around 7 million guys playing for a couple of hours a day, conservative estimate). Others are caught up in sports, TV, and banal jobs to the extent that when they finally have some time to relate, they're pretty clueless. There are some exceptions, like farmers' kids and guys who had good role models or who've figured it out for themselves and are really ready to go. But I don't think you should look for these needles in the haystack. Instead, I would suggest using your relational strengths to help develop us into better people. Remember, unconditional love is not about finding someone ready for you.

Commitment?
Alex: I freaked out because the "seriousness" hit me, even though it's not really serious at this point. We've only talked about the relationship and hung out for a weekend together. But it's like I have cold feet before a wedding, even though I know that that day is still far away, if ever.

Don't try to answer the question (of whether you want to commit) too soon. You don't know enough to process it, so don't even try. Just focus your creative and emotional energy on developing the friendship. After a while, you can come back to the question of commitment.

Alex: If I'm developing a friendship, we shouldn't really talk about emotions and stuff right? Do you think I should just let her continue to believe that I don't have any feelings for her, until I one day decide to tell her if I can commit to her?

Don't be too concerned about what she knows about how you feel. It's not important until you want it to be, and that's when you are ready to DO SOMETHING with the emotions. As in, commit yourself. Talking about the emotional stuff with her is premature. You have a lot of other things you can talk about. People try to lock in the deal way too quickly. Why is it so important now? She'll know that you like her, fine. But if you put language to it that you're not ready to follow up on, you'll really confuse her. Teenagers like sharing their emotions 'cause it makes them feel like grown-ups. Adults pace themselves based on their ability to commit. Keep it simple.

John: I understand that relationships are hard work, but are they supposed to be all hard work? Does any of it come easy? Or is this just another sign that I'm probably not supposed to be in it? For the last six months or so it seems like more of a duty than something enjoyable; is this normal?

There are no signs from above, unless God has singled you out of six billion people to lead your particular relationship. Probably not gonna happen so don't get superstitious and use it as an excuse to bolt. I am so freakin' tired of that. Anyway, relationships are not all hard work, but they all have hard seasons and, depending on our level of baggage and issues to be worked on (and theirs), there can be chronic stuff that seems to take years. You'll find this in any relationship: uninformed optimism followed by informed pessimism. You're probably in the informed part. This is the time to be a really good friend. If you're looking for a good time, you'll jump from relationship to relationship until something "pans out" (mining term, right?).

When you're working on your own selfishness and learning to be that amazing friend, there is a lot of joy and fulfillment. Maybe not the titillating kind we've become accustomed to, but a deeper kind that lasts a lot longer. I think one of your problems is that you're in a "relationship" and this is complicating it with expectations that you were never ready to be part of, at least not completely. So yeah, don't go backwards, get closer, but as a friend. Find that joy via giving and listening and contributing from your strengths, like your humor and kindness, and be facilitating.

Nathan: *I could be single forever, waiting for that "perfect" relationship to come along, and then wake up one day realizing that it actually never showed up. I would be a fool to keep looking, so should I just choose somebody along the way?*

Looking for perfection is a selfish waste of time. It pushes the "desire system" of our brain to such an extent that when you find someone even close to what you wanted, they can never fulfill you because desire is stronger than fulfillment. It's a dead end. I think what you're looking for is to be a committed person, not a person on the hunt. In this way, yes, you do choose someone along the way that you create love with. As long as your values line up with that person's, you can make up the rest of the relationship along the way. It's taken Heather and me these 25 years to develop a real love; what we chose in the beginning was the *potential* for that love to develop.

Shared values?
Nathan: Instead of the typical criteria (she's hot), what should I look for in terms of values? Are you saying we could marry whoever we choose and "create love" with them?

You're looking for both of your values to line up. What's super important to you about life, God, and priorities. And if your values line up, yes, I think you could create love with just about anyone. Not everyone, but I also don't think God has one person chosen for us. I think you could marry thousands of different people, because this stuff isn't predestined, it's what you create with them.

Nathan: That's it? Are you saying that marriage is based on reason alone?

No, not just logic, but a love you create with your values and a heart for that person. Your soul is heavily involved as well as your mind and your neurotransmitters. Your emotions have a lot of triggers, for a lot of reasons, and are not meant to be at the top of the list.

John: The four criteria from 2 Corinthians (fellowship, harmony, agreement, and faith). Are these values we should look for in making a commitment?

Yes, not just these four, but they're important. Do you have agreement about things like children and money and the care of your parents? Do you have harmony about where you want to live and work? Do you have fellowship in terms of faith and acceptance of each other's diversity? A friend of mine married a person who did not share their faith, and it worked out because they did share just about everything else. Not every value is a deal breaker, but some are, and you need to know the difference before you get serious with someone.

Maria: Can interests be values, or are they different?

Interests, like sports, cooking, and wearing tight black clothes, are not values.
Values are things like:
- do you want children, how many and why?
- how do you treat money and why?
- would you care for your parents or his parents in their old age?
- are you an international person or a local?
- what does God mean for your life, calling, values?
- what are roles in the home, in a family, what's your role?
- what else is super important to you, the non-negotiable stuff?

God's role?
Helen: How much do you believe God is involved in all this?

I think God coaches us on how to be friends and what love looks like. He does not choose people for us; that's a lazy approach to God's part and it avoids our responsibility to walk out the principles.

Helen: But do you think God cares at all who we choose?

Not like we often think He does. We can think God has someone FOR ME (selfish). Or that He knows what's best FOR ME (selfish and afraid to be hurt). Or that He has someone who will complement MY MINISTRY (selfish and weird). Or that He has planned out my life and there is only one person who will fit into that plan (selfish and fatalistic). I think God cares about *how* we love (with faithfulness, integrity). I think God cares that we choose a whole family, not just their child. I think God cares how we grow that love into something that represents His values on earth as they are in heaven. The rest, He simply enjoys because we have free will.

Should I get married at all?
John: I'm 32 years old and for the first time finding myself in something that could evolve into a serious relationship. I think I am realizing that it's surprisingly hard to change my mindset from being single to being in a relationship at this age.

Yeah, being a little older is going to make this harder because you've created a groove for yourself which may now feel threatened, so you're looking for something extraordinary to break you out of this. You have to be careful because this can lead to a deep-seated selfishness that's hard to recognize due to the years of practice. An unconditional love seeks the best for the one you choose. You choose because you love, not for what you can get out of it. The choice itself is the primary form of love, not the feelings, not the response you get. It's the power to set someone aside and give yourself to them.

John: About that deep-seated selfishness you mentioned. Do you mean like looking for a superwoman to fill all my needs? Or what?

The older we get, the more we set things in place to stay happy. Commitment is a risky business, and when you don't take that risk earlier in life, you become cautious and selfish in the little things. We also need to take into account how we've been getting our needs met. If they're met by the love of God flowing through us, then we'll approach relationships in a centrifugal way. If we are not getting our needs met (unconditional love, provision, value, destiny), then we'll look to others to be that for us (like marrying someone to be your mom). The expectation for them to meet our needs is the beginning of the end of the relationship.

Nathan: So I had a talk with my parents last night, and it actually came surprisingly naturally. My dad was very indecisive before their wedding, and at one point they actually called it off. It helped him that some other guy also liked my mom, so he finally figured out what he wanted.

Cool to hear about your talk with the folks. I wish everyone did that! Seriously, just opening up the subject and hearing each other—very healthy. I don't think your dad's experience needs to be feared as a family bondage; it's a human condition, it's called shopping. It's when our criteria hit real-world opportunities and we're not sure that we want to "invest". It's not something you're going to inherit; simply find a better way and make that your lifestyle.

Nathan: In some way marriage will have to improve my life, right? Or else I would not deliberately walk into this.

So, you'll only get married if it improves your life? The whole opportunity of marriage is to bless someone else. How much can you give? What capacity do you have for another? And children? And extended family? Can you see how selfish we've become in this whole approach? It's no wonder so many people are taking forever to get married. They use up all their options as singles and then leech off someone else for the rest of their lives. When love or value flows through us to others, it meets our need for love and value. If they return it, great, but our core needs are met through the generosity of friendship, love, and commitment.

Nathan: Okay Patrick, I think you have to explain to me why you think marriage is a good thing. We can love unconditionally as singles, so then what's the point of getting married? Especially when marriage looks like a lot of pain and hard work and so many marriages end up in divorce...

I think you can *give* more as a married person than you can as a single. You can give to your children, to your partner's family, to your grandchildren... This will challenge your selfishness daily. Being single, you choose when you want to be giving or not. Marriage will improve you as a person in deep ways. And yes, a lot of marriages do fail, which is why I'm writing this book. They're hard work but, at the same time, they're immensely powerful and fulfilling. I don't think you *need* to be married to be an amazing person, but personally, I'm convinced I would not be half the man I am without the marriage I'm in.

Andrea: Wouldn't you say that "you complete me" is good in the sense that the strengths of the one will improve the weaknesses of the other and in that way make them better people by challenging their weaknesses?

Iron does sharpen iron and you're right in that we complement each other with our diversity. But the "you complete me" thing can be a pop-psychology trick. You're already complete as a person. No one *needs* to be married (okay, I lied, men need to be, women don't). What we need is to create together. We will complement each other in different ways, so I'm not totally in disagreement with Jerry Maguire or love languages. Complementarity is something we forge over decades. We just have to turn off the radar that's always searching for someone to complete us.

Andrea: I agree, I just remember being interested in someone who was almost completely like me, and that was annoying. It's always good to challenge one's boundaries, don't you think?

Yes, commitment forces the issue. When we commit ourselves, even to be friends, we start rubbing against things that irritate us or challenge our world view. This is how we learn to be ourselves and still love the diversity of others. Imagine doing that over 30 years with someone.

Going too far?
Maria: In expressing my emotions toward a friend some time ago, we created an atmosphere of heaviness where the ease of friendship turned into an emotional wall between us. I know I can't take back the weirdness now, but I desperately want to become friends again or for the first time.

The consequences of rushing things is that it creates a kind of scariness that people don't wanna go back to. Especially guys. In your situation, I would suggest being honest with him. Without any pressure for him to respond emotionally, tell him you want to be a good friend and want to find a way to make that happen. The key to this working is that you both have a Godly understanding of friendship and how to get there. Friendship is a relationship we develop over years, so give yourself time. This will allow you to ease off any residual attraction-based motives for pursuing him.

Maria: But how I can handle the emotions or bring them to an end? Especially so I can act towards him without any hopes or expectations. A good friend suggested I cut off the relationship, but if feels like I'd be running instead of dealing with it.

I think you have a very good perspective on this and it shows your level of maturity and strength. In terms of what to do with the emotions, I think you have to accept that you're attracted to him for good reasons, things you like about him and appreciate, and that's fine. It's awkward that he knows you feel more, but that's okay. You're both adults and can deal with it over time.

In terms of your heart though, it needs an opportunity to ventilate the emotions. Tell God how you feel about this guy and how you appreciate him. Ask God to show you how He thinks of this guy. Your emotions are fine and it's disappointing that he doesn't share how you feel, but if you want to love him, or anyone, it has to be for their sake and not for yours. So accepting that he wants to move on is how you love him. If your heart can only be fulfilled by him responding to you, then you are stuck. The power of love is when you use your emotions to motivate yourself to be committed to his best, whether that's with or without you. It will be painful, but if it's love that you feel, you can use that love to release him if that's what's best. Plus, if you can release him (which it sounds like you have) and still commit to being a good friend, you'll have reached new depths in yourself that will be adding strength and grace to your life. This kind of grace is all you really need, and honestly, it's the only way to build lasting relationships.

Alex: How do I follow up the revelation that the relationship I'm in is, and was, a mistake?

Dating may have been a mistake, but I don't think the friendship is. Stay good friends, get closer, not further apart. If you've had any heart for her, don't lose that. Backing out now will never teach you how to learn from your mistakes. Why should she have to pay for your expediency? Go forward with what you're learning and don't use it as an excuse to cut out and be "free". You have to be honest about where you're at but you should also be able to be a better friend from this point on. And be careful not to rush into some other relationship to compensate for this.

Helen: I've been in a long-distance relationship for a few months. We're both sure that we wanna get married sometime in the future. We grow together, we pray together and have the same goals in life. But there's one thing that keeps being a problem when we do get together; lust and physical intimacy. The thing is, I don't know what's wrong and what's right anymore. I mean, where do we draw the line? Who says that kissing is okay and everything else isn't? I feel like we're just following some rules that I don't even understand myself. At the same time, I don't want this to destroy our trust...

There are a few things to consider. Some of it you're already past, but allow me to go over it properly as it may help next time. 1. Sounds like you started the relationship too fast. You guys probably should have known each other longer, simply as friends. Because as friends, you don't have the permission to get that physical. It can still happen, but you're not setting yourself up for failure by calling it love, or a relationship.

2. The issue with being physical is simple. If you're not committed, you shouldn't be physical. And commitment means marriage. There's no in-between commitment, like, "I'll date you and then kiss you and stuff, and then see if I want commitment 2.0". That's lame. And here's the real problem: if a person can't control themselves before marriage, then they're showing that they probably can't control themselves after marriage. If this is what they are willing to do now, then they don't understand real commitment and self-control, and would probably be equally stupid later.

3. Don't fool yourself and think that if it's real love, it's okay to get physical. If it was real love, he'd be committed and marrying you or have the self-control to honor you (and your families). You're "pretty sure" you want to be married, but until you actually are, anything can happen, and often does. Don't be naive with each other.

4. Another reason you need to be careful is that you're vulnerable. If you're not getting your needs met in a healthy way (through family, committed friends, God), then you are way too open to this subtle form of abuse. Work on this as a top priority. Also, when you're together, make sure you have people around you to help. Be honest with your friends and family and ask them to help you be accountable. It's not about being religious, it's about understanding commitment and self-control so that you set foundations for the rest of your lives. People that are willing to rush into things often don't have the strength to go the distance. If you guys are growing spiritually together, one of the fruits of that should be self-control, right? Work on the areas of

your vulnerability and this will decrease the openness to being taken advantage of, even if you like it.

Finally, I think you do know, in your heart, where the line really is. Try to find the reasons it gets blurry. Is it that you don't want to lose him? Is it fatherlessness? Is it simply a matter of pleasure and lack of self-control? You have a lot of wisdom and all the grace you need if you call it into action. I guess the biggest thing at this point is to talk to your parents and friends and put things into the light. Just that alone will bring a lot of clarity.

———————————

I'm sure you have ideas about all this and different points of view or more questions. Come check out the site and let's keep the conversation going. http://www.patrickdodson.net/relationships

Breinigsville, PA USA
11 October 2009
225630BV00004B/25/P